CYBERNETIC PSYCHOLOGY AND MENTAL HEALTH

This book explores the cultural importance of cybernetic technologies and their relationship to human experience through a critical theoretical lens.

Bringing several often-marginalized histories of cybernetics, psychology, and mental health into dialogue with one another, Beck questions common assumptions about human life such as that our minds operate as information processing machines and our neurons communicate with one another. Rather than suggest that such ideas are either right or wrong, however, this book analyzes how and why we have come to frame questions about ourselves in these ways, as if our brains were our own personal computers. Here, the rationality underlying information theories in psychology is followed to its logical conclusion, only to find it circles back to where it began: engineered methods of human control. After tracing a series of recent developments in this vein across fields related to mental health, Beck highlights emerging psychosocial alternatives by incorporating recent work of scholars and activists who have already begun creating collective support networks in radical ways. Their work overlaps fruitfully with ideas from those, including Gilbert Simondon and Fernand Deligny, who foresaw many of the current problems with how information theories have been coupled with psychology and mental health care.

This book is fascinating reading for advanced undergraduate and postgraduate students across psychology, mental health programs, and digital media studies, and academics and researchers with a theoretical interest in the philosophy of technology. It's also an interesting resource for professionals with a practical interest in organizing care services under the data-driven imperatives of contemporary capitalism.

Timothy J. Beck is an Assistant Professor of Psychology at Landmark College. His research takes a critical, transdisciplinary approach in exploring how social boundaries are both regulated and persistently reconfigured through applications of psychological theories to problems related to "mental health."

Concepts for Critical Psychology: Disciplinary Boundaries Re-thought
Series editor: Ian Parker

Developments inside psychology that question the history of the discipline and the way it functions in society have led many psychologists to look outside the discipline for new ideas. This series draws on cutting edge critiques from just outside psychology in order to complement and question critical arguments emerging inside. The authors provide new perspectives on subjectivity from disciplinary debates and cultural phenomena adjacent to traditional studies of the individual.

The books in the series are useful for advanced level undergraduate and postgraduate students, researchers and lecturers in psychology and other related disciplines such as cultural studies, geography, literary theory, philosophy,

Most recently published titles:

Rethinking Education through Critical Psychology
Cooperative schools, social justice and voice
Gail Davidge

Developing Minds
Psychology, neoliberalism and power
Elise Klein

Marxism and Psychoanalysis
In or against Psychology?
David Pavón-Cuéllar

For more information about this series, please visit: https://www.routledge.com/

CYBERNETIC PSYCHOLOGY AND MENTAL HEALTH

A Circular Logic of Control Beyond the Individual

Timothy J. Beck

LONDON AND NEW YORK

First published 2020
by Routledge
2 Park Square, Milton Park, Abingdon, Oxon OX14 4RN

and by Routledge
52 Vanderbilt Avenue, New York, NY 10017

Routledge is an imprint of the Taylor & Francis Group, an informa business

© 2020 Timothy J. Beck

The right of Timothy J. Beck to be identified as author of this work has been asserted by him in accordance with sections 77 and 78 of the Copyright, Designs and Patents Act 1988.

All rights reserved. No part of this book may be reprinted or reproduced or utilised in any form or by any electronic, mechanical, or other means, now known or hereafter invented, including photocopying and recording, or in any information storage or retrieval system, without permission in writing from the publishers.

Trademark notice: Product or corporate names may be trademarks or registered trademarks and are used only for identification and explanation without intent to infringe.

British Library Cataloguing-in-Publication Data
A catalogue record for this book is available from the British Library

Library of Congress Cataloging-in-Publication Data
A catalog record has been requested for this book

ISBN: 978-0-367-25293-9 (hbk)
ISBN: 978-0-367-25294-6 (pbk)
ISBN: 978-0-429-28704-6 (ebk)

Typeset in Bembo
by codeMantra

CONTENTS

Preface — vii
Acknowledgements — ix

Introduction — 1

1 Towards a technical history of thinking about human thought — 8
  Introduction 8
  Technology as a medium for thinking about human thought 11
  The cybernetic foundation of current methods of psychosocial control 15
  Some social reasons for the research-practice divide in psy-disciplines 18
  (e)Merging overlaps across technoscience, data collection, and mental health 21

2 Cybernetic narratives beyond *The Individual* — 25
  Introduction 25
  First-order cybernetics: engineering an impulse for psychosocial control 27
  Rethinking mental health in terms of second-order ecologies 31
  Gilbert Simondon and the role of affective modulation in transindividual networks 36

3 Three (psycho)logical myths of auto-
  individuation (pseudo-AI) 45
  Introduction 45
  Psychoanalysis and the myth of psychic-individuation 49
  Behaviorism and the myth of operant-individuation 55
  Cognitive neuroscience and the myth of cerebral-individuation 66

4 Deinstitutionalization, biopolitics, and
  network maps of "mental disorder" 77
  Introduction 77
  From deinstitutionalization to the decentralization of mental health 80
  Biomedical neoliberalism and the ongoing cooption of deinstitutionalized care 86
  The edges and nodes of new computational diagnoses 99

5 Disorder without borders 104
  Introduction 104
  Protocological control and the dividualization of mental health 109
  Pre-individual investments underlying concepts of mental health 115
  Circulating diagnoses as social currency 120

6 The network as a mode of being 124
  Introduction 124
  The techno-politics of hacking 129
  Identifying the glitches in mental health programs 133
  From collective self-advocacy to network subjectivities 139

References 149
Index 163

PREFACE

The over-optimistic mantra of the internet was that "information wants to be free," but it turns out that machine-organised circulation of information in capitalist society entails that human beings are anything but free. And, this book shows us, the discipline of psychology is into this problematic from the neck up, eagerly re-circulating cybernetic metaphors in each and every modality, whether that be behaviourist, cognitive, or psychoanalytic. There is a particular specification of the individual within such regimes of truth, and a specification of what kind of society must be put in place to house them, to enable them to work, for us to imagine that we are happy and healthy. On the one side is the implicit programme of psychology, programming each of us to adapt to these new conditions for knowledge-production, to become self-regulating individuals. These conditions, and the images of the individual they enforce, are carefully unravelled, deconstructed, in Timothy J. Beck's scholarly analysis as the "myths of auto-individuation" that lock us into place, ensuring that we know our place. On the other side of the viciously circular individual-social equation is the explicit programme of surveillance and regulation of our lives, whether sitting in front of the screen or asking for help of a psychologist for how to cope with these conditions. Here we are in the realm of "societies of control," and here we need conceptual anchor-points to grasp what is happening, those provided by Gilles Deleuze and Félix Guattari, neatly complemented in this book by the descriptions of individuation and technology provided by Gilbert Simondon.

We urgently need to take a step back from the peculiarly restrictive specification of individuality and society provided by cybernetics, and this is what this book, *Cybernetic Psychology and Mental Health: A Circular Logic of Control Beyond the Individual*, does. It enables us to disentangle ourselves from the mechanistic universe of adaptation and control, and to bleach out the alluring colourful fantasies that so-called "Artificial Intelligence" provides researchers and practitioners of psychology; while it is, indeed, "artificial," the machine-processing of loops of information is anything but "intelligent," and to claim more for it than it warrants is also to devalue what embodied collectively organised human beings bring to the world in their creative labour and their reflexive understanding of the world, reflexive understanding that does not merely repeat the shape of the world but also aims to transform it for the better. Here are the highest stakes of the book, how we are to find a better way to think about distress, one that is very present in cybernetic theory and in present-day programmes of "global mental health."

This book is much more than a grim and necessary analysis of the problem; it maps out solutions that are already present on the most progressive edges of psychological practice, those that go beyond cybernetic rationality to build what the book describes as "collective networks of transindividuation." Whether it is from within interventions organised around the notion of neurodiversity or inside networks of those who hear voices and reclaim their experience for themselves, we need to work in the "liminal" spaces available to us, inside psychology and outside it, reconceptualising who we are and what we may be, "outwith" cybernetic rationality, beyond, radically "surplus" to it.

Ian Parker
University of Manchester

ACKNOWLEDGEMENTS

There are far too many people involved in the creation of this work to do justice to everyone. However, I want to extend special thanks to my fellow graduate students, teachers, mentors, and students during my time at the University of West Georgia, where I was continually challenged to rethink old assumptions and reimagine psychology in new forms. It was in the courses I took with Hans Skott-Myhre, Lisa Osbeck, John Roberts, Alan Pope, and Kareen Malone that the ideas across this book began to take form; ideas which were gradually refined with the help of my amazing cohort, including Emaline Friedman—whose critical feedback on this text was invaluable—as well as Jake Glazier, Nick Atlas, Chris Biase, Chris Bell, and Robert Beshara. Then there were the discussions about technology with Andi Winderl, language with Marie-Cécile Bertau, transhumanism with David Mitchell, and hypermodern pathologies with Ayurdhi Dhar. Beyond the daily conversations spanning philosophy, technology, psychology, and social theory—which I will always miss—the sense of community I found at UWG transformed me in profound ways. I would also like to thank Sammy Nelms and Trei Hill. Our conversations about art, technology, media, and psychology were constant sources of inspiration during the writing of this book. Both of you humble me with your creativity and are friends in the truest sense of the word. Finally, I want to thank my partner, Kristi, for putting up with me during the years I spent working on this book and the dissertation that preceded it. I could not have finished this without your love and support.

INTRODUCTION

The emergence of cybernetics research during the middle of the 20th century represents a culmination of Western civilization's quest to create a universal language of scientific knowledge. One-by-one, processes underlying living and non-living systems became translated into a common framework of *information* and *communicative control*. Academic research has since become wedded to public policy and private interests in ways that could not have otherwise been possible. Cybernetic metaphors extend across psychosocial research, psychiatry, and other mental health professions—despite those working in such fields remaining largely unaware of the cybernetics movement itself. Anytime the mind is characterized by its "information processes," for instance, or groups of neurons are said to "communicate with other areas of the brain," cybernetics is evoked. It is all too easy to forget, however, that such phrases are conceptual heuristics, not scientific facts. Despite providing robust metaphors for plugging individual bodies into material environments and social systems, certain possibilities for thinking, feeling, and acting are inevitably foreclosed when all interactions are reduced to processes of explicit communication between separate individuals (see Hayles, 2001).

Rather than propose that cybernetics either is or is not the best model for thinking about systems in general, this book narrows in on how and why it has come to influence so many different areas of human life. Several histories are traced in the text below, but they are not organized in a conventional, linear fashion. Some overlap chronologically; others chart events occurring before or after the cybernetics movement reached its peak. With the wide range of fields covered in this text, it is unquestionably a transdisciplinary endeavor. And yet, a critical and sustained focus on how ideas related to psychology and 'mental health'[1] have been reconfigured through lenses stemming from cybernetics remains a constant theme throughout. In this way, American society during the 20th century can be characterized by an overarching drive to program into machines traits that have traditionally been considered exclusive to humans, reframing the boundaries around each in relation to the other in increasingly idealized, mechanistic forms.

Today, this drive is fueled by a growing variety of ways psychological methods are used to collect data on individuals' thoughts, emotions, and behaviors. In a world where person-centered data informs industry practices, online cultures, and daily habits, the control and measurement of individuals' experiences have become highly valuable for a wide range of social institutions. This has, in turn, incentivized the interpretation and reinterpretation of data about mental health such that new information networks have emerged across otherwise distinct professions. The theories and narratives analyzed throughout this text each provide an example of a certain form of administrative logic underpinning these expanding networks—a notably fluid form of collective organization that Gilles Deleuze (1992) refers to as *societies of control*. Here, "what is important is no longer either a signature or a number, but a code: the code is *a password* … that mark[s] access to information or rejects it" (p. 5). This is the language of cybernetic rationality (see Halpern, 2014), where putting symbols in the correct order determines entirely which social opportunities are made available for someone. While control is not inherently a bad thing, and as Deleuze suggests, language itself operates by ordering the world according to certain social structures, control can become dangerous when it is the goal of social action rather than the means. At the same time, danger implies indeterminacy—a possibility for something unforeseen. As this book argues, it is only in the liminal spaces between conventions of social order, on the one hand, and emergent social movements, on the other, that the limits of cybernetic control, specifically, can be identified and overcome.

After sketching a general outline of what is at stake in this book in Chapter 1, Chapter 2 explores the historical significance of a range of tech-orientated research programs that emerged in the middle of the 20th century. This brief history of cybernetics highlights critical points of intersection across psychology, data-collection, and mental health care. Insofar as cybernetics was the result of intentional attempts by engineers, social scientists, and psychiatrists to construct a universal language of systemic control, its influence can be seen across nearly all fields of research today. Because the digital tools developed from this research possess such high degrees of social utility, this influence likewise extends far into government and throughout the tech-industry.

Rather than simply focus on the broader implications of the cybernetics movement, however, Chapter 2 analyzes some micro-dynamics of the social contexts where early cybernetic principles were developed. Discussions between those interested in cybernetics early on reveal incredibly prescient ethical and conceptual tensions regarding how digital technology can and should be used to alter human life. A central concern for these groups was the role of the observer in any social situation, with a particular emphasis on research settings—the way that each researcher enacts a certain frame of reference that can condition research through the way terms are operationalized, certain tools are used, and data are interpreted based on prior research. This has important practical implications in terms of how psychological theories translate to social practices like mental health care and organizational management. Although psychology and psychiatry have always been notably different professions, cybernetics bridged them together through a common conceptual framework whereby all behaviors and brain activity could be translated uniformly into digital processes of symbolic exchange.

Finally, Chapter 2 explores new possibilities, limitations, and alternatives for cybernetics through a discussion of Gilbert Simondon's theory of technology and general psychology. Simondon was one of the great scholars and early critics of cybernetic research during the middle of the 20th century. Deleuze (2004) noted Simondon's unique display of "intellectual power with a profoundly original theory of individuation implying a whole philosophy" (p. 86). It is, indeed, Simondon's preoccupation with rethinking the individual in a manner that transcends conventional subject/object relations that makes his theory of technology so revolutionary. The importance he places on thinking theoretically through the individuation of technical objects according to their relations with physical bodies and groups offers what is perhaps an even more timely set of insights today than it ever could have been when he was alive.

Chapter 3 builds upon this history of cybernetics *vis-à-vis* three foundational theoretical frameworks in psychology: psychoanalysis, behaviorism, and cognitive neuroscience. More specifically, it examines how each of these frameworks constructs a certain notion of "a self-regulating individual" (e.g., the psyche, the organism, and the neuron), each of which has been used, in turn, to map constellations of imagined, known, and unknown relations across bodies and social contexts. From psychoanalysis to behaviorism, and even with cognitive neuroscience, the goal of researching such concepts has been to identify causes for human behaviors in ways that, once revealed, allow for more effective control over them. With psychoanalysis, causes for behavior are situated within each individual psyche, and the analyst is tasked with interpreting symptoms as signs of an unconscious architecture. With behaviorism, on the other hand, such causes are externalized into the environment, despite remaining largely unconscious to the organism. In this framework, the behaviorist researcher holds the correct formula for identifying such causes and intervening on the organism's behavior accordingly. And in cognitive neuroscience, neural networks are mapped in increasingly visual forms, creating a concept of the unconscious in the form of an abstract constellation of binary mechanisms, arguably pushing it even further outside of everyday life than it had been under behaviorism.

Pursuing this logic even further, then, the conceptual systems formed between psychological frameworks and notions of "the individual" are analyzed as social technologies, insofar they are used to translate bodily processes into mechanistic, or otherwise functional, terms whereby they can be more easily controlled and communicated about according to broader systems of socioeconomic value. It has been common for such psychosocial systems, or *myths of auto-individuation*,[2] as they are referred to throughout the book, to be repurposed by social institutions for a range of purposes. Each psychosocial system, as it were, allows for a certain set of relationships between terms and bodies, that would otherwise not be observable, to be measured and mapped in ways that can effectively shape such relationships from that point forward. In this sense, they operate as ideologies of "the individual" that form practical feedback loops with experimental settings, allowing data and concepts to be reinterpreted in relation to each other on an ongoing basis.

Returning to cybernetics, the paradigm shifts from psychoanalysis to behaviorism and later to cognitive neuroscience can thus be understood as a series of stages towards the digitization of the unconscious, encoding it into formulas that become artifacts used to enact greater degrees of control over humans and machines. Importantly, this correlates with analogous changes to the primary clinical tool used by mental health professionals, the *Diagnostic and Statistical Manual for Mental Disorders* (DSM). It, too, has become more digitized—through its differential coding schema—over the same historical timeline. In these ways, theories and categories underpinning how mental disorders are classified, researched, and treated have become increasingly abstracted from the lived processes to which they are supposed to refer.

Overlaps between psy-disciplines and cybernetics are outlined more explicitly in Chapters 4 and 5, illustrating a steady historical progression towards a cybernetically organized system of mental health care. Starting with the deinstitutionalization of psychiatry in the mid-20th century, mental health services have steadily become more mechanized through biomedical knowledge and cybernetic metaphors in ways that have extended their practical applications to a growing variety of social settings. This corresponds with significant changes occurring during the same period across the five main versions of the DSM, where it has been transformed from a manual based in psychoanalytic theories, with explanations of behavior in terms of early childhood experiences, to a growing set of descriptive categories with no explicit reference to any conceptual framework. In this way, the DSM has become more easily appropriated across a broader range of social institutions for purposes other than those it was created to fulfill.

These chapters also focus on how the changes described so far can be linked to what some researchers have described as the neo-liberalization of mental health care. Here, culturally relative boundaries are drawn not only around groups of individuals (e.g., ethnic groups, nationalities, genders) but also around discrete diagnoses and individuals themselves, distinguishing them from one another through cybernetically organized attempts to assess and manage various forms of risk. This underscores some problematic consequences of deinstitutionalized mental health care, insofar as the decentralization of services has made the psychological myths of auto-individuation outlined in Chapter 3 pre-packaged for ever-wider distribution around the world. Unfortunately, this often occurs without regard for the concerns and tools of local cultures, or social context more generally.

Cybernetics has remained at the basis of these processes in several different ways. With the translation of the world into series of code, human thoughts and behaviors can be more effectively decoded and recoded into terms that can, in turn, be more easily controlled and communicated about. Not only does cybernetics provide a useful set of theoretical principles for rethinking the history of psychology and mental health care, but the information technologies it has produced allow professionals to talk about "mental health" in ways that would not otherwise have been possible. Beyond the traditional goals of social engineering, cybernetically organized clinical research facilitates broader capitalist purposes related to mass data-collection and storage, as such networks can, in turn, be repurposed by corporations and government agencies to improve machine learning architectures of their AI networks. This brings more general ethical issues concerning data-collection and privacy under the purview of clinical psychology in ways that few mental health professionals have begun engaging with directly.

Chapter 6 points to potential alternatives to biomedical approaches to mental health care by drawing on projects carried out by collectives already engendering psychosocial care in highly creative ways. By analyzing the issues described so far through the social character of "the hacker," the metaphor of psychological theories as social technologies is extended up to, and beyond, its logical conclusion. The hacker is invoked to illustrate how self-advocacy and other user-rights movements are both facilitated and complicated by theories in psychology being more widely distributed across not only social institutions but, perhaps more importantly, virtual social media platforms. Groups like neurodiversity (Kapp et al., 2013) and the hearing voices network (HNV) (Hearing Voices Network, 2020)—both of which are comprised largely of self-advocates creating alternatives to corporatized biomedical models of mental health—make significant use of online forums, blogs, and other virtual mediums to share resources and coordinate collective action. A common theme across these groups is that they experiment with psychological terminology playfully for unique personal and political reasons, often in ways that cut across established social boundaries and challenge institutional control. This is proposed as a form of hacking the psychological myths of auto-individuation described throughout the rest of the book.

The concept of the network as a mode of being, as such, serves as a cultural corrective to the universalizing data-driven trends common within contemporary capitalist markets. Rather than designating categorical labels around which behavioral treatments might be carried out, or consigning a disorder entirely within an individual, glitches in a system are interpreted as opportunities to rearrange the sociomaterial conditions through which groups are organized according to a yet existing (in)formation of living together. Such diagnostic ecologies are discussed in terms of what Guattari (1995) refers to as *collective assemblages of enunciation*. Situating Guattari's work relative to that of Simondon and other cyberneticians, these movements can be understood, alternately, as *collective networks of transindividuation*. Rethinking care practices in terms of processes of transindividuation, *ala* Simondon, as opposed to the prediction and control of individual behaviors, *ala* cybernetics, would have important ethical and conceptual implications for the array of subject groups involved.

The respective projects of Simondon, Deleuze, and Guattari are brought together in this book insofar as they each offer important insights with respect to sensing and mapping the often-subtle variations of material movement undergirding social networks. Each thinker underscores, in a unique way, how the individuation of persons and things can only occur through synergistic processes that assemble and differentiate otherwise disparate elements through relations with each other. Their writings, especially when understood together, foreshadow what are currently some of the most pressing concerns regarding how psychosocial relations are increasingly mediated through technical metaphor and quantitative formula. More specifically, therefore, an overarching goal with this book is to trace a transdisciplinary framework, based on a critical history of cybernetics in psychology, that underscores alternatives to current psychosocial drives to control, collect data on, and ultimately profit from the behaviors of others'.

Notes

1 I use the term "mental health" here hesitantly in reference to the professional fields that use it as a signifier, and not some ideal standard of psychological well-being to which all individuals should strive.
2 There are, of course, overlaps here with Thomas Szasz's (2010) characterization of "mental illness" as a myth that is used to exert sociopolitical control over deviant individual behavior. To be clear, however, the way the word myth is used throughout this book is not necessarily meant to be pejorative. By myth, I simply mean a narrative structure that, similar to Freud's theory of drives, illustrates the underlying architecture through which social groups are organized. In this sense, myths have certain productive capacities that can account for their popularity or lack thereof.

1
TOWARDS A TECHNICAL HISTORY OF THINKING ABOUT HUMAN THOUGHT

Introduction

Information about what others might be thinking has become an increasingly valuable commodity within contemporary capitalist societies. Private companies employ market research strategies in ever more inventive forms, hoping to discover what we want, desire, or think we need. Psychologists and other mental health professionals are continually reviewing information about individuals in the forms of notes, assessments, and research studies to more effectively intervene on their thoughts and behaviors. And what are social media platforms other than corporatized, digital ledgers of personal thoughts, opinions, and reactions, which we add to every time we logon? The sheer breadth of these concerted efforts to probe more deeply into the nature of human experience points to something beyond a mere amplification of prior attempts to establish greater scientific certainty about the world. They express qualitatively new obsessions with accumulating *information about information*, whereby assumptions about "mental health" are reconfigured through channels of social communication that are themselves able to be tracked and communicated about. While concerns related to surveillance and privacy are of course important here, a more general set of questions relate to how datasets collected on humans are "fed back" into the mechanisms by which we understand ourselves in relation to what we perceive to be the world. This renders mediation a fundamental principle in such societies, as perception in general becomes increasingly dependent on networks of information technologies (e.g., an internet of things) and the users who subtend them.

And yet, there are unavoidable limits to thinking about thinking—underscoring conceptual, practical, and ethical questions about how data collected about human life can to be interpreted and used. Such limits have traditionally been framed through a notion of *access* to information, referring specifically to who has been granted access and to what extent. In a purely phenomenological sense, for instance, we cannot directly access others' thoughts in the same way we do objects in the world. This is also true, in a slightly different sense, for our own thoughts. Philosophers have described such issues in terms of first-person vs. third-person perspectives, the *hard problem of consciousness* (Chalmers, 1997), or the "problem of other minds" (Leudar & Costall, 2004). With social organizations today relying on personal/behavioral data more than ever before, however, information about what others could be thinking has become valuable for reasons outside of academia. Under the totalizing conditions of global capitalism, such data cannot possibly be collected and mobilized in ways that can be made accessible to everyone equally. In economies where the demand for networked data rivals that of material goods and services, overlaps across market research, biological sciences, and diagnostic assessment yield value primarily for individual entities with the technical capital required to access and analyze said data.

This book explores how conventional problems regarding *who* has access to *what kind* of information have been reconfigured, broadly, for new social purposes that cut across issues related to mental health, governance, and technology. At the basis of each of these social arenas are new demands to map the ways certain populations of individuals think, behave, and/or feel. New network approaches to psychopathology, for instance, are being used to organize growing banks of mental health data into computational models, transforming diagnoses from pre-defined categories to evolving constellations of biological, psychological, and social traits (see McNally, 2016; Jones et al., 2017). Despite all the talk lately about data-ethics across industries and sciences generally (Kostakis & Bauwens, 2014; Ekbia & Nardi, 2017), very few mental health professionals or clinical researchers have questioned how the collection of such data might have consequences for service users moving forward. This has broad social relevance not only because of the way policies and funding are so intimately tied to scientific research—although this is an important point also addressed below. Even more relevant to what has been discussed so far, however, this signals how mental health professionals have begun turning to the same technologies that are already being used to surveil individuals around the world and, by extension, organize data collected on them into ever more comprehensive information infrastructures (Halpern, 2015; Mayer-Schönberger & Ramge, 2018).

These examples illustrate how datasets about human thoughts and behavior are not simply collected for their own sake; today they are often mobilized to intervene on behavior across diverse domains of social life (Zuboff, 2019). This has consequences well beyond the goals for which psychological data collection practices were initially developed. Whenever concepts like *the individual*, *mind*, or *culture* are used to surveil and intervene on social behaviors, for instance, their meanings tend to taken-for-granted and, in most cases, tailored to conform to the overarching social purposes of institutions employing these methods. This is reminiscent to how the privileged position traditionally afforded to the concept of humanity, on the one hand, and the boundaries between human bodies and machines, on the other, have been challenged by recent movements like posthumanism and transhumanism (see Ferrando, 2014), with new theoretical frameworks proposed that are better equipped to engage with global problems unique to the 21st century. Critical analyses of how ideas in psychology are inextricable from social values are thus useful not because they chart absolute boundaries beyond which thought is impossible, or even because they reveal essential qualities about human nature. Rather, by marking the conceptual mechanisms underpinning current modes of society, life itself can be reimagined in forms that would otherwise be unthinkable given the most popular socioeconomic values.

More specifically, critical histories of psychological practices, particularly those associated with the term "mental health," provide robust case studies for thinking through the ethics of emerging techno-governance models and how subjectivities are produced through information networks, as such. This is evident in the way research on humans, most notably in neuroscience, depends increasingly on innovations in digital technology, as well as how technical metaphors are applied so liberally to explain poorly understood areas of human life. This is likewise important in terms of reflecting more generally on how the margins between humans and machines, as well as individuals and groups, are steadily redefined through information processing tropes so that data about "mental health" can be more easily integrated into transdisciplinary research programs. Here, it is necessary to account for how what would have been considered purely academic concerns in earlier generations are actively incorporated into the decision-making processes of transnational companies and governments around the world. Theories about human psychology and mental health are thus unavoidably structured through conditions of contemporary capitalism, where ethics is often but a subsidiary of overarching goals like risk-assessment and financial growth. With emerging network technologies being employed by mental health professionals, researchers, and service-user activist communities alike, there has never been a more important time to interrogate how data and information about "mental health" is collected, stored, and interpreted, and reflect critically on who benefits from its mobilization, as such.

Technology as a medium for thinking about human thought

From Aristotle's notion of the mind as the navigator of a ship to the hydraulic model of the psyche proposed by Sigmund Freud, there is no shortage of metaphors throughout Western history that link technology to human thought. Rather than attempt to determine which of these are the most useful today, this book explores the social affordances technical metaphor provides within particular places and times. There is one technical framework that stands out as especially central to the history psychology in general: Rene Descartes' *mechanistic* theory of science (see Schultz & Shultz, 2015). What is arguably one of the first myths of psychological auto-individuation emerging from scientific research, Descartes' dualism famously separated the mind and body into two, completely different realms of reality. Human bodies were said to operate according to natural laws of the physical universe, and it was the task of scientists to uncover the logical mechanisms underlying human action. This is also the domain where animal behavior resides. Data collected on bodies through experimental studies were expected to conform to such laws and, when they did not, it was typically an indication of error on the part of either the scientist or the tool used for measurement.

Human minds in Descartes' framework, by contrast, were granted privileged access to God—at least to the extent their thoughts remained rational. Following his model to its logical conclusion, individual minds can only learn about the world outside of itself through a reliance on God, as the chief programmer of the physical world. This is how Descartes was able to wed science, ideologically, with religion—as scientists were said to have special insight into the mind of God. What makes Descartes' philosophy even more relevant to the concerns of this book, however, is the way he linked God to mathematics, subordinating both mental and physical processes, albeit in different ways, to the same ideal mathematical structure. Here, divine principles and mathematical principles were fused into uniform, universal laws of nature. And in this way, human minds were uniquely positioned to comprehend the extended universe of which their bodies operated as physical parts.

This, in turn, formed the foundation of Descartes' representational theory of knowledge, whereby the truth value of any idea an individual might have is determined solely by its capacity to mediate between the most essential parts of an object, or body, affording a predictable degree of control over its organization. Gilbert Simondon (2013) underscores how this was a core aspect of Descartes' epistemology of mind. With:

> Cartesian mechanism, the fundamental operation of the simple machine is analogous to the functioning of logical thought capable of being rigorous and productive… [where] the transfer of forces goes from link to link, so that if each link is welded well and there are no gaps in the enchainment, the last link is fixed to the anchoring point in a more mediated but also more rigorous way than the first. (p. 2)

In this way, the analytic nature of modern knowledge, as formalized by Cartesian geometry, links the organization of life axiomatically to the conditions of thought, such that "if [living beings] were not machines *ontologically*, they would have to be so at least *analogically* in order to be objects of science" (p. 3). Simondon furthermore describes Cartesian mechanism, in this sense, as a particular cognitive schema—a schema of intelligibility—by which a certain form of technical thought made it possible for scientists to represent human thinking with "no gaps in the enchainment." In other words, with no scientific method available to access human thought directly, scientists have traditionally been able to learn about mental processes only by comparing them to something already situated within the realm of scientific knowledge—e.g., technology?

Well before artificial intelligence (AI) became a popular conversational trope, it was common for psychiatrists and psychologists to construe individual persons in terms of mechanistic systems composed of functional relations. Making sense of human beings through technical metaphor has such a long history in Western thought that it is almost impossible to talk about conceptual innovations in psy-disciplines (i.e., psychology, psychiatry, and psychotherapy) without considering contemporaneous ones in technology (Leary, 1994). Comparisons have been made, for instance, between Freud's theory of the psyche and the steam engine (Carveth, 1984), but he was perhaps fonder of the "mystic writing pad" as a model for memory traces and the unconscious (see Freud, 1925). The influence of electrical engineering on the thinking of Skinner and other behaviorists was clear with the broadly construed switchboard model they used to map organism–environment relations mechanistically as stimulus-response circuits (Edwards, 2000). And of course, applications of digital computing metaphors to the human brain, and by extension, the mind, has made possible all sorts of systems diagrams of human thought and action across social domains as diverse as medicine, education, and war (see Boden, 2008).

To date, clinical researchers interested in mental health have engaged, at best, indirectly with ethical issues related to computer–human interface. The focus tends to remain exclusively at the level of the individual, where there might be expressed interest, for instance, with effects of social media use on mental health, or with how human cognitive capacities can be enhanced through technical devices. As alluded to above, the most innovative research in this domain incorporates ideas that developed out of former cybernetic programs, which now range from social network theories to neural networking. And yet, there are many noteworthy examples of psychiatrists and psychologists across the 20th century who were concerned primarily with systems and how individuals operate within them. As I outline below, several enduring figures, in fact, laid the theoretical foundations for trends currently cutting across data-driven industries, information sciences, and mental health care. By theorizing about networks of cause and effect beyond the scope of individual persons, historical figures like Sigmund Freud and B.F. Skinner provide prescient insights regarding current impulses to decode individual behavior as a function of their environment.

As Keller and Longino (1996) suggest, moreover, understanding the role of the individual in relation to the environment is important for reasons beyond the important contribution of *standpoint theory*, moving into a critique of "the supposed universality of scientific norms" (p. 3). Going further, they explain how concepts like dualism, consciousness, and the individual are each shaped uniquely by the historical constraints placed on science at any given moment, which includes the tools scientists have at their disposal. Haraway (1996) describes, for instance, how the even concept of:

> The "eyes" made available in modern technological sciences shatter any idea of passive vision; these prosthetic devices show us that all eyes, including our own organic ones, are active perceptual systems,

building in translations and specific ways of seeing, that is, ways about life. (Haraway, 1996, p. 254)

In these ways, the tools used to collect and analyze data condition not only what we are able to measure but also how we ask questions about and, even, perceive what the data is supposed to represent. Exploring scientific research from the perspective of the "researcher as person," as Osbeck (2018) suggests, emphasizes that science-based activities are unavoidably structured by a range of personal and social values that cannot be entirely isolated and controlled for through the scientific method alone.

These overlaps across the practical and theoretical dimensions of science are especially relevant today given the increasingly data-driven nature of most professional pursuits. Organizations ranging from colleges to banks rely on data about individual behavior to make decisions about how their finances and resources should be managed, rendering digital technology essential to their underlying institutional infrastructures. Similar developments can be seen in academic research programs as well. Research in nearly every discipline relies on computers to store and evaluate data in ways that mediate relations between humans and the world. Here, aspects of human thought that would otherwise remain unobservable can be represented (hence visualized) in new, ever-more elaborate forms. The most widely funded studies on humans are, for instance, typically in neuroscience, where conceptual innovation relies on ever more creative applications of computers to elicit new neurological data, which are then fed into the development of new neural maps. And in mental health contexts, new computational models of mental disorders have been positioned as viable alternatives to conventional diagnostic taxonomies like the Diagnostic and Statistical Manual for Mental Disorders, or the DSM (see McNally, 2016). Data collected about individuals' mental, social, and biological lives are being plugged into network modeling programs that map constellations of traits in ways that can continually be updated as more data is collected on service users (see Jones et al., 2017). In these ways, Cartesian mechanism has become refined in ever more practical forms through the models of "mental health" we use to think about each other and ourselves. This can be seen even in cases where Descartes' mind-body dualism has ostensibly been transcended through materialist explanations for human behavior, like contemporary neuroscience, for instance (see Damasio, 2005). And yet, his mechanistic approach to science continues to condition how human knowledge is wedded to both technical artifice and empirical data.

The cybernetic foundation of current methods of psychosocial control

Many of the most popularly discussed issues related to machine–human interface can be traced directly to the cybernetics research programs of the mid-20th century. During this period, concepts like communication, information, feedback, and recursion—analogues of ideas psychologists had been theorizing about for decades—were redefined by academics, industry professionals, and psychiatrists collaborating across disciplinary lines (see Pias, 2016). Methods and concepts spanning the fields linguistics, biology, and engineering were brought together under the assumption that physical processes underlying organic systems can (and should) be mapped, coded, and decoded in the same terms used to understand inorganic systems. Even philosophy and the humanities have been transformed through cybernetic principles and metaphor (Hayles, 1999). The idea of a cybernetic self—as a machine–human cyborg—for instance, became a common 20th-century trope across domains ranging from science fiction, the social sciences, and tech industries (see Haraway, 1990), hence the popular understanding of cybernetics as something related to computers and/or robots. It is not an overstatement to say that cybernetics has left a lasting mark on nearly every area of academic research.

Etymologically, the term cybernetics can be traced to the Ancient Greek term *kybernetes*, meaning "steersman," which was often used metaphorically for purposes of state governance. While 20th-century cybernetics certainly has this implication, this research applied the notion of governance liberally to almost all areas of the universe. Here, the most important differences between orders of reality (e.g., molecular, psychological, social) are no longer qualitative but quantitative, represented in terms of the degree of self-organization observed in a system. Simondon (2013) describes such early cybernetic programs as offering a much more fluid cognitive schema than Descartes's philosophy. More specifically, with cybernetics, it becomes possible to rethink relations between physical elements in terms of a new concept of "relay apparatus," forming "the basic schema that allows for an active adaptation to a spontaneous finality" (Simondon, 2013, p. 3). For Descartes, the power of any research method depended on its ability to accurately predict the position of each element, *a priori* to any particular moment in time, within a given series of physical effects. Cybernetics, on the other hand, presents an altogether different epistemology, whereby temporal processes can be tracked uniquely in "real-time" and mapped as modulations across what are ultimately indeterminate possibilities.

This involves a form of causality that is distinctly different from Descartes' model of the universe, or what Gilles Deleuze (1990) has described as a *quasi-cause*. Here, effects of systemic processes (e.g., data) can develop a capacity to double-back onto their causes (e.g., experiments) and influence them in what appears from the outside to be non-linear ways. With this, continuous feedback in the form of *information* becomes an overarching determinant of action in "self-organizing" systems. This relatively new, cybernetic schema of causality has since been applied to networks of a growing range of scales, shapes, and material forms. Cybernetic research programs of the middle 20th century have, moreover, provided the conceptual foundations for current programs of machine-learning (Shannon, 1971)—tools that are used today to produce computer models of networks ranging from neuronal assemblies to diagnostic symptoms and cultural groups. And yet, despite the robust history of applications of cybernetics to social problems, the term itself is not usually considered more than a footnote within research on information networks and digital technology.

The most ubiquitous legacy of the cybernetics movement could be the concept of information itself. Maintaining a system of governance based on the continuous collection and transcription of data is substantially easier in a world in which everything of relevance can be translated into the terms of information theory. Donna Haraway (2000) illustrates this phenomenon by comparing how:

> [i]n communications sciences, the translation of the world into a problem in coding can be illustrated by looking at cybernetic (feedback-controlled) systems theories applied to telephone technology, computer design, weapons deployment, or data base construction and maintenance... [with] modern biologies [where] the translation of the world into a problem in coding can be illustrated by molecular genetics, ecology, sociobiological evolutionary theory, and immunobiology. The organism has been translated into problems of genetic coding and read-out... In a sense, organisms have ceased to exist as objects of knowledge, giving way to biotic components, i.e., special kinds of information-processing devices. (p. 303)

The concept of "cyborg semiologies" described above points to a semblance of a universe composed entirely of overlapping, tightly networked circuits of input–output exchanges (i.e., functional variables), offering a ready-made blueprint for professionals to navigate any problem that might emerge in their work. Social risks identified across what would otherwise be different social contexts can in this way be sequenced and redistributed through commonly coded protocols that operate through cybernetic principles of information feedback and communicative control.

There are countless ways in which cybernetic principles can be seen "feeding-back" into a broad range of psychosocial practices, particularly with growing popularity of cognitive-based research, practices, and therapies. Here, the human mind has been reconstructed in the form of an information processing machine, calculating risk and reward from one social situation to the next. If nothing else, such trends serve as useful case examples of the degree to which thinking about the thoughts, emotions, and behaviors of others in terms of functional relations of varying degrees of order and disorder has become the default approach across business, educational, and healthcare settings alike. The use of cybernetic metaphors, like earlier technical analogies, afford heuristic purposes for researchers in ways that cut across academic disciplines, while providing a vocabulary for the value of scientific concepts to be more easily translated into social purposes beyond academic institutions.

By integrating cybernetic tropes, like the information processing model of the mind, into its own theoretical repertoire, psychology has evolved in ways that allows it to be plugged into new social problems. Similar to the cybernetic research programs during the mid-20th century, methods and concepts from psychology today are commonly applied to collect data on humans for a range of public and private interests (Zuboff, 2019). With research methods and data being shared so often across academic and non-academic settings, however, it is worth asking if the unit of analysis remains the same even if the social values around which the practice is arranged changes. In other words, whenever psy-concepts are applied outside of academic or clinical settings, does the unit of measurement remain "the individual," as defined by psychology, or does it become something else? In lieu of asserting that theoretical frameworks used in psychology should be judged strictly on the basis of whether they are true or not, cybernetics allows them to be assessed according to the technical utility they afford within complex psychosocial systems.

Such essential overlaps between psy-disciplines and cybernetics evoke important questions about the social and epistemic values tying psychological research to mental health care and other social practices, beyond their bases in scientific research. Cybernetics provided psy-practitioners a new set of conceptual tools—primarily information and feedback—that allowed subjectivity to be situated explicitly within social networks in ways that were previously only implicit in their methodological decisions.

With arenas of human life ranging from industry and war to medicine being translated into information processing tropes, the definition of concepts of mental health through cybernetics made it possible, in turn, for them to become more widely distributed and embedded within the goals and values of a growing variety of social institutions (Zuboff, 2019). One of the primary tasks of the current book, therefore, is to explore what might be gained and, alternately, foreclosed by reading the history of Western psychology—and by extension, mental health practices—through the lenses of cybernetic frameworks.

Gilbert Simondon, in particular, offers a prescient take on how psychology must be reimagined with the emergence of digital information technologies. Foreshadowing current discussions about AI and consciousness, he granted all technologies a certain sense of agency in relation to humans in ways that diverged markedly from most of his cybernetic contemporaries. For him, while humans are irreducible to automatons, they are simultaneously more and less than individual in ways that trouble traditional boundaries between individuals and groups, and technology and culture. And yet, he never gave up on the concept of humanity entirely, always keeping human culture *human* even if human existence remains dependent on something other than itself (e.g., technology). This book reinterprets the history of psychology and mental health with the help of Simondon's concept of transindividuality, whereby individual bodies are designated with capacities to be projected towards networked possibilities beyond themselves. This concept of sociomaterial synthesis is further situated in relation to both a history of cybernetics and contemporary information technologies, with a particular focus on how they have influenced psychological research and mental health care.

Some social reasons for the research-practice divide in psy-disciplines

Psychology has long been understood as a discipline with an identity crisis (Heidbreder, 1939). Throughout its history, one theoretical framework or another has been borrowed from outside of the discipline as a potential unifier, with neuroscience serving as the most popular choice as of late. This likewise points to the complicated relationship between psychology and psychiatry, especially as it relates to mental health care. While the two are clearly different disciplines, with different assumptions, concepts often creep seamlessly across such boundaries, with neuroscience serving as the bridge connecting them together. This has become especially relevant following the deinstitutionalization movements of the mid-20th century. As institutionalized psychiatric settings were closed across the Western world, mental health care became a concern for a growing number of social institutions and professions. This includes settings like schools and private companies, where topics like "emotional management" and "cognitive load" are commonly incorporated into pedagogical and management strategies (van Bruggen et al., 2002). In these ways, psychiatric care has become reconfigured in terms of distributed systems of mental health services, with notions from psychology, psychiatry, and neuroscience integrated into general frameworks of human management that stretch across medical and non-medical settings alike.[1]

The current book argues, in fact, that concepts from psy-disciplines have historically proven socially useful precisely because they do not easily conform to a single set of disciplinary prescriptions. Throughout psy-disciplines, theories have linked concepts together in ways that have allowed them to be applied more easily to social problems. Psy-theories, as such, operate as social technologies insofar as they can be tailored to meet the information needs of increasingly wide range of social institutions. This has become especially relevant since the deinstitutionalization of mental health care. With psychiatric hospitals closing across the country, mental health services became packaged in ways that can be easily transferred from one setting to another. For the same set of concepts to be employed across contexts as diverse as schools, psychotherapeutic settings, and corporations, for instance, it makes sense for them to be easily tailored to specific demands of each setting in which they are used. Histories of concepts in psy-discipline illustrate how they have always been wedded inextricably to social and/or professional purposes that transcend purely scientific concerns.

For these reasons, the structure of the Diagnostic Statistical Manual of Mental Disorders-5 (DSM-5) (APA, 2013), as well as specific diagnostic categories, can be understood in terms of what Star and Griesemer (1989) refer to as *boundary objects*. According to these authors, boundary objects are any set of conceptual technologies that, rather than serving as stable reflections of an essential physical nature, possess qualities of being "both plastic enough to adapt to local needs and the constraints of the several parties [involved]… yet robust enough to maintain a common identity across the sites" (p. 393). As for categories of mental health and disorder, for example, there is an unavoidable vagueness, or interpretive flexibility, to them that functions to simplify communication at the boundaries of distinct disciplines and professional contexts (Allen, 2009). This in turn allows for high degrees of practical and communicative utility even if the concepts and theories with which such technologies are packaged remain, at best, works in progress.

Insofar as the contours of categories of psychopathology are shaped to correspond to specific information needs of social institutions at which they are employed, their usage—and hence meaning—is nonetheless conditioned by the conventional orders of procedural organization (i.e., protocols) that allow them to link successfully with other institutionally specific boundary objects. These are cultural artifacts—general map—that provide enough interpretive flexibility to be used at the boundaries of distinct disciplines and social contexts. Going further, they can contribute relatively coherent sociomaterial assemblages—composed variably of theoretical constructs, information technology, and institutionally specific mission statements—forming progressively more comprehensive structures of socioeconomic organization. Star and Griesemer (1989) refer to these as *boundary infrastructures*. Encompassing insurance companies, big-pharma, big-data, and academic institutions, the corporate-academic hybrid structure that is the biomedical industry (see Gomory et al., 2011) can be understood as just such a cybernetically organized boundary infrastructure, insofar as the ways that diagnostic categories are used often conform to broader informational and economic needs of these institutions.

Cybernetics has played an essential role in these developments, as well, with neural networks and information processing models of the brain and mind providing conceptual links between fields of research in psychology, sociology, and biology that might otherwise not make sense in relation to each other. Here, cybernetic metaphors provide useful conceptual vehicles to interpret data collected on human systems and non-human systems alike according to a common set of systemic principles. However, as with the ontological impasses discussed above, crossing communication gaps from the human to the non-human is neither a straightforward nor value-neutral move. Cybernetics has never been promoted as a mirror of nature—it is a set of technologies that, from the beginning, have been used to enact control over the component-parts of targeted systems. Such concepts are not inherently problematic; yet they can become so insofar as they are deployed to collect data on humans for reasons that prioritize social institutions over individuals themselves. With information processing metaphors circulated so commonly across social institutions today, diagnostic instruments and manuals operate as data collection tools that facilitate with more complex information processes of social and professional negotiation. This in turn renders mental health care practices uniquely situated to be appropriated by a broad range of organizations for purposes like tracking, recording, and modifying behaviors (see Luxton, 2015). In these ways, diagnostic categories can be hollowed out and used to transmit information about social risk around signifiers that would otherwise refer to individuals.

With clear causes for psychopathology difficult to come by for clinical scientists (Karter & Kamens, 2019), viable alternatives to the DSM have emerged recently, several of which are overviewed below. A promising example is the Power Threat Meaning Framework (Johnstone et al., 2018), proposed by the British Psychological Society, which critiques not only the DSM but also the biomedical model and cybernetics frameworks that underpin its ongoing organization. Alternatively, they recommend an approach to mental distress based in peer-support and user knowledge, positioning the concept of *narrative* in a central role in ways that allow more comprehensive clinical portraits painted of any given person's experiences. As these sorts of approaches become more popular around the world, definitions of terms related to psychology and mental health are destined to be pushed up to and past their conceptual boundaries and repurposed by service users as well as organizations for their respective purposes.

(e)Merging overlaps across technoscience, data collection, and mental health

Relationships between mental health and technology have become some of the most popular topics of conversation in psychology today. The focus here, however, tends to be on improper uses of digital technologies and how to pathologize individuals' relationships with them. Recent examples include the World Health Organization adding digital gaming disorder to the 11th revision of the International Classification of Disease (ICD) (Gaebel et al., 2017) and the APA recategorizing non-substance related behaviors, like video gambling, together with substance-use disorders in the DSM (Potenza, 2014). Ignoring the cultural specificity of human tool use in general, the growing use of digital technology is all too often framed as a threat to humanity writ large, with the autonomy of individuals constrained through a growing dependence on a certain class of technical objects. However, this book argues that such attempts obscure the extent to which culture, technology, and psychology are materially inseparable and, in fact, always have been.

In these ways, every technical innovation serves as a Rorschach test for broader social imagination. As we are pushed collectively to reconceive ourselves through the new technologies at our disposal, the boundaries around what we consider "possible" and even "real" are extended in ways that feed into higher expectations for social performance and self-sufficiency. Today, this is fueled by mounting compulsions to collect as much data as possible on human behavior. While it is common for such data to be mobilized for reasons that involve shaping others' thoughts, emotions, and/or actions to specific social ends (e.g., through marketing or user research), relations between humans and data have likewise come under public scrutiny more than ever before. Topics like AI, data mining, and data-security populate news headlines around the world. Professionals across nearly all industries, particularly health care and education, are hard-pressed to stay up to date with the latest evidence-based (i.e., data-driven) recommendations.

At the same time, the speeds at which new technologies used to collect data on us become integrated into everyday life render their social implications impossible to assess prior to their popularization. This renders anything resembling ethics an almost impossible task. At any given moment, the average person is engaged in hundreds of contractual agreements related to apps, websites, and technical software, with the terms of accessing such technologies written in highly codified language that few who use them are equipped to understand. Typically, this serves to obscure the extent to which such technologies are actively collecting data on their users. There is simply too little time and, seemingly, too little interest to question exactly how the massive amounts of data collected so far—more than could ever be analyzed in a single lifetime—might have already reshaped our understanding of ourselves, much less how it might be mobilized for purposes beyond the profit-motive. Insofar as data already collected on human behaviors guide decisions across a growing variety of institutions, it is imperative to think critically about how data-management practices and the technologies undergirding them spur us to relearn, on an ongoing basis, how to navigate the shifting social fabrics underlying contemporary life (Ekbia & Nardi, 2017).

Research in psychology occupies an increasingly important role in such data collection practices (Zuboff, 2019). As illustrated in more detail below, applications of psychology to social concerns in this vein rely on two, closely related cybernetic concepts: *modulation* and *control*. It is here that digital technologies, on the one hand, and information processing metaphors, on the other, have transformed the ways we think about *mental health*. Mental health practices, in this sense, can include those directed by care providers—in clinical settings, for instance—but also networks of support, advocacy, and solidarity formed across service users operating outside of such institutions. I further explore how notions of order and disorder are negotiated across these social domains through analyses of (a) historical research in cybernetics and psychology, (b) contemporary programs for mental health treatment, and (c) the social performance of mental health through online forums. Drawing on contemporary service user movements (see Parker, 2014), "mental health" is understood thus here as a particular set of historically situated discourses and social practices rather than an ideal standard toward which individuals might strive.

Contemporary approaches to mental health have developed complicated relationships with traditional scientific values like empirical evidence and data collection. On the one hand, care providers place a great deal of esteem on notions like "empirically supported interventions" or "evidence-based practice," rendering previously conducted scientific research a guiding determinant of how each client is treated in any given case. On the other hand, the systems through which such services are coordinated circulate ideas about mental health in ways that push them outside of clinical institutions, collecting behavioral and medical data across a greater variety of social situations. The growing use of mental health apps in everyday life is but one example of this (see Huckvale et al., 2019). In such ways, digital technology—as both a set of tools and an overarching metaphor—occupies progressively more central social roles in discerning health from illness, what is normal from what is perverse.

And yet, the inverse of this relationship, with unrealized visions of new technologies framed in terms previously reserved for human traits (e.g., intelligence, attention, perception, sensation, etc.) is perhaps an even more psychologically provocative trend. Humans and technologies are no longer merely models for one another; their evolution has become intertwined conceptually and materially through processes that authors like Ekbia and Nardi (2017) refer to as "heteromation" in contrast with earlier modes of automation. Some implications of this are evident in how corporations, universities, and government agencies apply data-collection techniques (i.e., "data-mining") to individuals' internet activity to in turn improve their abilities forecast and manage institutional risks. Control over social groups is, for them, a byproduct of broader economic incentives to mobilize information on humans in ways that either improve machine-learning capacities of their AI systems or create funding streams allowing their respective research programs to continue.

At the very least, such practices point to important shifts in our collective imagination regarding our relationship to technical objects, as such. Beyond the worn-out trope of humans being overly dependent upon machines, we seem to have reached a point of irreversible interdependence where the developmental trajectories of digital technologies depend on the growing amounts of data collected on each of our everyday activities (Ekbia & Nardi, 2017). As Luciano Floridi (2014) describes, this trend is likely to lead to "new ways of conceptualizing ourselves, our world, and our culture hyperhistorically and informationally, no longer historically and mechanically" (p. 218). At this current sociohistorical juncture, both real and imaginary boundaries between nature, humans, technology, and culture are destined to be pushed to their limits, deconstructed, and refashioned, with resources from otherwise failing social institutions repurposed to support the lofty data-collection goals of corporations, nongovernmental organizations (NGOs), and national governments.

Note

1 Mental health professionals like Beth Stroul et al. (2008), for instance, advocate a *systems of care* model of coordinating services in the community as "a complex, multilevel process with goals and outcomes at various levels of intervention" (p. 3).

2
CYBERNETIC NARRATIVES BEYOND THE INDIVIDUAL[1]

Introduction

What has come to be known as *cybernetics* began as a loosely connected set of research programs stemming from concerns related to machine–human interface and communication at the basis of World War II. These programs coalesced into a concerted movement through a series of conferences that started in 1946, sponsored by the Josiah Macy Foundation—an organization that, according to its website, macyfoundation.com, has been working since the 1930s to fund research to improve healthcare and education in America. The first few of these meetings were known as the Macy Conferences on "feedback and circular causality in biological and social systems" (Scott, 2016, p. 502). With the publication of Norbert Wiener's 1948 book, *Cybernetics: Communication and Control in the Animal and the Machine,* however, the conferences were officially rebranded under its more popular moniker: Macy Conferences on Cybernetics (see Hayles, 1999). In the years since, direct links have also been confirmed between the Macy Foundation, cybernetics, and the Central Intelligence Agency (Pickering, 2016), with conference organizer Frank Fremont-Smith often referenced as a common nodal point linking the three (Kline, 2015).[2]

While most of the ideas discussed at the Macy Conferences can be traced to earlier theoretical developments in physics, biology, and psychology, what made the discussions there unique was the overarching, collective intention to reconfigure conventional boundaries between not only academic disciplines but also organic and inorganic systems in general. Wiener (1965), in particular, sought to construct a common technical language of systemic organization, which could be tailored to any field of research, and to position the vernacular of cybernetics as a foundation for a new science, bridging areas of study that have for too long:

> been explored from the different sides of pure mathematics, statistics, electrical engineering, and neurophysiology; in which every single notion receives a separate name from each group, and in which important work has been triplicated or quadruplicated, while still other important work is delayed by the unavailability in one field of results that may have already become classical in the next. (p. 2)

Demonstrating a prescient interest in transdisciplinarity, Wiener made sustained efforts to collaborate with researchers across disciplines to combine concepts and address concerns that transcend any single field of study. He was convinced that underlying all complex systems are common theoretical principles—such as negative feedback and self-organization—which could be described and measured with similar methods regardless of observed scale of the system.

The theoretical frameworks stemming from the Macy Conferences have since been applied to assemblages ranging from computer networks and robotics to general electric circuits, groups of molecules, and even social systems (Umpleby, 2008). The most obvious legacy of cybernetics is information theory, despite the way circular causality is often ignored within applications of the latter (Kline, 2015). While these might initially appear to be quite different domains, each requiring its own method of analysis, cybernetic metaphors have been applied indiscriminately across them all to map underlying structural dynamics that are otherwise unable to be observed. This can be understood, as such, in terms of an ideology of technology, where myths of auto-individuation presuppose relations between terms that are "self-organizing" despite the way they are interwoven with their environments as well as the observer who is analyzing them.

Gilbert Simondon described cybernetics as an innovation on par with the creation of modern philosophy. And yet, he firmly emphasized that there are inherent limits to applying cybernetic principles and metaphors to make sense of human thoughts and emotions. While many of these limitations were noted earlier by other cybernetic theorists, like Mead, Bateson, and Von Foerster, none of their proposed alternatives are as comprehensive as Simondon's concept of transindividuation. For Simondon, individuals—whether they be objects, concepts, or organic bodies—can only become what they are, gaining any sense of unity, through the relations they *form* with everything around them. Such a never-ending process of becoming one thing in relation to another is described, quite aptly, as in*form*ation. This is especially true for individuals, which are never fully developed and as such cannot be represented in terms of a static state. In the context of what has been discussed so far, this theorization of information is especially important considering how psychological theories about individuals are crafted within professional contexts with cybernetic discourses, but then become distributed, *ala* forms of media, across an array of digital and non-digital cultural platforms.

Rather than simply being an extension or alteration of cybernetic research approaches, I suggest Simondon's philosophy of technology offers an avenue towards the development of a new general psychology, insofar as his method and concepts situate the discipline of psychology within a more critical framework of technical evolution. Given how concepts in psychology are used across many social contexts today to intervene on mental health, this, in turn, elucidates key insights about the organization of contemporary mental health care. This sets the stage for discussions in Chapter 3 where Simondon's critiques of cybernetics are applied to proto-cybernetic theories in modern psychology. This also foreshadows discussions in later chapters where I outline several possible relationships between cybernetics, digital technology, and emerging network forms of psychosocial care. The concepts overviewed in this chapter are thus repurposed as a set of critical analytic tools used throughout the rest of the book to deconstruct historical developments cutting across various psy-disciplines and contemporary social institutions.

First-order cybernetics: engineering an impulse for psychosocial control

According to psychologist Bela Julesz (1971), the "era of cybernetics and information theory is marked by the study of complex systems with stochastic input signals and the measuring of stochastic output parameters" (p. 153). For Bernard Scott (2016), what makes a model "cybernetic" is its ability to represent causality circularly, as with the operation of a thermostat, as opposed to linearly, as with one pool ball striking another. And yet, there is perhaps no more comprehensive definition than the one offered by Norbert Wiener (1989) in his book, *The Human Use of Human Beings: Cybernetics and Society*. Here, Wiener links cybernetics directly to the control of human communication, encompassing:

> ...not only the study of language but the study of messages as a means of controlling machinery and society, the development of computing machines and other such automata, certain reflections upon psychology and the nervous system, and a tentative new theory of scientific method. (p. 15)

Wiener reconceived language in general in terms of a complex matrix of communicative codes, with control over such codes representing a "problem" to be "attacked" with a combination of technical and conceptual tools. Indeed, one of the primary reasons that cybernetics can be considered a notably distinct theoretical schema from those before it is the way it linked control—epistemically and instrumentally—to linguistic practices and social interaction writ large. In this way, social control and communication were reconceived such that they can continue to refine each other through feedback mechanisms formed between them. In theory, this allows organisms to evolve by staving off the natural processes of decomposition that would otherwise erode upon life.

Coupling social control and communication in this way likewise allowed Wiener to situate the concept of information as a core feature of cybernetic theory. Information, in the sense used by Wiener, is simply the process through which units of data are structured into meaningful wholes—arranging them, quite literally, in *form*-ation. Wiener argued that such a cybernetic framework, once properly articulated, could provide a new technical toolset for scientists and engineers to decrease disorder within any observed physical system. From this perspective, disorder can be construed as *entropy* and represented by data input into any system at a certain scale of observation (e.g., chemical, biological, social, etc.). Information can thus be contrasted with entropy as order with disorder—whereas information refers to the degree of organization measured within a system, entropy refers to the degree of observed disorganization.

Such a functional, inverse relationship posited between information and entropy was fundamental to Wiener's thoughts on psychology, particularly his theory of motivation. For him, information is essentially "a name for the content of what is exchanged with the outer world as we adjust to it, and make our adjustment felt upon it" (Wiener, 1989, p. 17). This, in turn, presupposes a notion of reflexive agency that possesses a capacity to compare the effects of control enacted in a certain environment with what might have occurred otherwise, without anacting an "adjustment," as such. In other words, Wiener construed entropy in terms of "a function of the discrepancy between the current state [of an organism–environment system] and the goal state" (c.f., Deyoung & Krueger, 2018, p. 168). However, the goal state does not refer to any already actualized state; the future is simply yet processed data—entropy to be turned into information. From this perspective, all that exists is the present state and the immediately preceding one, which provides the continuous feedback necessary for goal states to be reconfigured over time. Hence, the "circularity" of the systems Wiener was interested in.

Starting from this fundamental distinction between information and entropy furthermore allowed Wiener to ground a notion of voluntary activity in the interplay between systems of varying scales—from physiological to environmental. For him, all embodied action in general can be reduced to a series of tropisms—spontaneous movements of growth in reaction to, or a turning towards, an arrangement of environmental stimuli. While this term, *tropism*, is typically reserved for vegetation, Wiener (1989) applies it liberally to all animal behavior illustrating how preferences in thought and behavior emerge as any organism learns about its own capacities in relation to environments. As he explains, "for in man we consider that a voluntary action is essentially a choice among tropisms" (p. 166). Progressively more complex hierarchies of temporality and purpose (i.e., cognition) emerge as overarching determinants of behavior when one tropism appears just as preferential as others. The sense of choice invoked here is, as such, dependent on a sense of time by which potential decisions can be ordered in terms of importance in relation to imagined goals that extend beyond the immediate context.

This information theory of cognition became the basis of Wiener's concept of *cybernetic control*, which—particularly when applied to humans—came to serve practically and logically as an extension of B.F. Skinner's notion of *operant control*. For both Wiener and Skinner, learned behaviors could be described as functions of their relations to environmental stimuli and the circuits of reinforcement formed between them (Pinto, 2014). One of the main differences between the two approaches being, however, that Wiener's information theory allowed for a form of negative feedback[3] beyond automatic reflexes through cognitive information. This allowed principles of conditioning to be adapted to the respective concerns of computational and neural sciences.[4] Particularly with the latter, cognition became a determinant of behavior in systems (e.g., organisms) that can self-regulate towards predetermined goals. Insofar an individual organism can perceive a discrepancy between its intended goal and its actual state, according to Wiener, information provides valuable feedback whereby organisms can reorient themselves in relation to changing conditions across environments.

On a broader level, however, it is important to recognize the extent to which Wiener's theory of cybernetic control requires a largely unaccounted-for observer to discern between information and entropy in a system and effectively categorize them from a third-person perspective. This is the sense in which Wiener's work, especially early on, operated at a *first-order* cybernetic level. This was especially true regarding his concept of the organism. Despite arguing that neurological activity is not a closed system, *per se*, he nonetheless posited a self-sustaining boundary around each individual organism, granting it a sense of closure—a singular purpose towards self-organization. Practically speaking, this made it easier to translate the observed operations of living organisms and digital computers into analogous terms that could be integrated into common empirical models. As Wiener (1989) explains, "the physical functioning of the living individual and the operation of some of the newer communication machines are precisely parallel in their analogous attempts to control entropy [i.e., the future] through feedback [i.e., the past and present]" (p. 26). This likewise invests each self-organizing system with a respective capacity for intelligence, understood simply as an ability to interpret information from a source external to oneself (i.e., data input) and transform it into a form that can be used at a later time (i.e., information output).

It is thus not very difficult to understand the relevance of cybernetics, with its emphasis on reliable communication, information feedback, and systemic control, for current topics related to digital technology and media. Not only were mid-20th century cybernetic theorists involved directly in the creation of early digital computers, ideas from the Macy Conferences continue to influence social domains ranging from cryptography to media studies (Clarke, 2014). At the levels of both technical innovation and popular culture, cybernetics has transformed how people around the world use, and understand themselves in relation to, digital technology—even though most people have probably never heard the word.

While there have always been areas of obvious overlap between cybernetics and psychology, the former has steadily supplanted the latter as the preferred framework for organizing social life. Perhaps to avoid becoming irrelevant, psychologists came to reproduce the theories and methods of cybernetics in their own image. Computational models of the mind or brain, for instance, are by far the most dominant psychological frames for thinking about thinking. Cyber-psychological schemas in this vein have continued to prove instrumental in developing a conceptual foundation for neural networking (Abraham, 2002) and machine-learning systems (Cordeschi, 2002). Each of these tools, in turn, has become used increasingly by psychologists to produce computer models of networks ranging from brains to cultures. What we have thus been left with is a widely dominant *information processing model* of psychology, while cybernetics as an explicit scientific movement has gradually faded from public awareness.

What is perhaps a more complicated set of relations to trace are those between cybernetics and mental health care. Given how ideas from the Macy conferences were circulated so widely across disciplines, however, not to mention Macy foundation's explicit emphasis on healthcare and education, it is unsurprising that psychiatric issues were a primary concern for participants there. The group included psychiatrists, neuroscientists, and anthropologists, who each brought a unique perspective to bear on discussions about how systems remain organized or not. Norbert Wiener, in particular, expressed a pervasive interest in how psychiatric issues could be translated into information processing language, such that, as Halpern (2015) describes, "[c]ommunication failure was, in [Wiener's] terms, the analogue to mental illness" (p. 67). If all thought processes can be encoded at multiple levels of communication—between neurons, individuals, social groups, etc.—and errors in action can be reduced to errors in communication, psychological disorders should be able to be decoded as breakdowns in communication at essential junctures within an individual system.

Rethinking mental health in terms of second-order ecologies

Norbert Wiener's first-order approach to cybernetics was, however, not the only model that emerged from the Macy Conferences. As the meetings progressed, the validity of such an overt information processing metaphor for human life became a common topic of discussion. This had a tendency to take on a meta-reflexive dimension, with attendees analyzing their own conversations through the cybernetic frameworks they had been developing. As Claude Pias (2016) explains, quoting Hans von Foerster, attendees came to observe how "the common component of [their] language lay…not on the 'verbal level' but rather 'in a sort of ethos within which tones of voice serve as a common currency of communication'" (p. 14). In other words, a shared culture of expression emerged across these meetings, forming an implicit frame of reference that guided interactions between participants. The series of conferences itself, in fact, came to be described by several participants in terms of an evolving cybernetic system, in which each contributor formed a constitutive, interlocking part.[5] For those like Bateson, Mead, and von Foerster, in fact, the question of the human observer—and "not just any human, but specific humans linked to each other and to the Macy Conference they helped to create" (Collins, 2007, p. 26)—was the most important legacy of the conferences.

From here, a more concerted effort began to emerge among some participants to distinguish between first-order cybernetics of *observed* systems, which was Wiener's primary concern, and second-order cybernetics of *observing* systems. The latter were marked by their self-referentiality and greater degree of complexity. Von Foerster (2007) describes the difference between first-order and second-order cybernetics in terms of going from "searching for mechanisms in the environment that turn organisms into trivial machines" to searching for "mechanisms within the organisms that enable them to turn their environment into a trivial machine" (p. 152). By the term "trivial machine," Von Foerster is referring to those whose operations are generally reliable and do not require radically new information to continue operating. Essentially, this represents a shift away from using cybernetics to shape (i.e., control) the behaviors of others, to implementing its principles reflexively, as critical epistemological tools, such that coherent relations can be perceived across otherwise unrelated environments.

As early as the 1950s, Bateson and a group of colleagues began applying second-order cybernetics to problems in psychiatry ranging from how knowledge is acquired about those seeking treatment (i.e., assessment) to how those seeking treatment acquire knowledge about their worlds (i.e., personal experience) (see Beck, 2020). In 1956, for instance, Bateson et al. (1956) proposed a new theory of schizophrenia based on communication patterns connected to what they referred to as *double-bind* scenarios. In lieu of reducing schizophrenia to problems within individual brains— the dominant approach to this day—the double-bind theory posited that symptoms of schizophrenia can be induced, or at least expressed, through relations between family members that, often unconsciously, reinforce irreducibly conflicting messages. Therapy from such a perspective would involve mapping such communication patterns onto the power dynamics already underlying each clinical relationship, such that alternative (more playful) modes of relating to others can be cultivated over time.

Bateson further developed these insights about second-order cybernetics and mental health in a 1971 essay on Alcoholics Anonymous (AA). There, he overviewed various popular characterizations of addiction while carefully noting common epistemological errors at the basis of each. Again, rather than focusing exclusively on the brains or minds of certain unwell individuals, Bateson (1971) argues that mental conflict in such cases can stem from certain assumptions many of us are taught about our bodies in relation to our minds from an early age. Namely, he points to the "Anglo-Saxon epistemological tendency to reify or attribute to the body all mental phenomena which are peripheral to consciousness" (p. 446). Connecting this more specifically to the Cartesian mind-body dualism on which most "Occidental" philosophies of subjectivity are based, he outlines similarly culturally relative problems with respect to how we are conditioned to compare notions of 'self' with distinct 'others,' with transcendent values like 'pride' serving to mediate between the two sides.

Bateson goes on to illustrate how key components of AA programs can induce correctives for such epistemological errors by, for example, promoting new performances of oneself in public—in front of trusted peers—whereby one's understanding of one's 'self' can take on a new meaning in relation to a range of others. Through these rituals, conventional narratives underpinning notions like 'self,' 'pride,' and 'others' are rearranged according to an alternative system of value defined as "God as you understand him to be" (p. 452)—a fundamental precept of AA. What is important here for AA, as much as for Bateson, is that such a conception of God as a "higher power" serves as an access point to, on the one hand, an actual community of supportive others and, on the other hand, the general ideology underpinning all AA programs. Stripped of any essential theological denomination and understood simply as a power greater than the "self," this access point is utterly unique for each person and presents opportunities for new orientations towards "others" that are symmetrical and complementary rather than aggressive—the latter considered to be the Occidental norm.

Implicit in Bateson's analysis is an altogether new notion of epistemology that, in turn, implies a similarly novel concept of mind. Although Bateson's cybernetic theory of mind, like Wiener's, presupposes a concept of information where each "bit" is "definable as a difference which makes a difference" (p. 443), the epistemic values underpinning second-order cybernetics depart markedly from the Wiener's emphasis on cybernetic control. With first-order cybernetics, behavioral elements of a system are encoded from a third-person perspective, with any goals for the system defined according to whatever parameters are assumed by the authorial observer—in the case of mental health care, the clinician or researcher.

Second-order cybernetics, by contrast, involves a critical, meta-cybernetic reflection on how such goals are defined, charting epistemic consequences that result from focusing on certain distinctions between behaviors and environments while ignoring others. The very act of making a distinction, in this sense, enacts a frame of reference by which information interpreted from that perspective will, in turn, necessarily be constrained—all according to the particular (in)form(ation) of that frame. If observers in such cases refuse to recognize their roles in making such distinctions, an ontological gap is artificially inserted between mutually constitutive threads of what is ultimately an interactive and iterative process.

This is not to say that AA is always the best option for those who abuse alcohol, or that the double-bind model of schizophrenia should replace all others. But Bateson's analyses of these two phenomena chart a new approach to thinking about mental health in general. Re-envisioning the organization of mental health care from such a critical, second-order perspective involves making explicit how social and personal values are embedded uniquely in each clinical encounter. Human behaviors develop over-time as constituent parts of complex networks of individual habit and cultural ritual. Outside of the most normative social settings, otherwise identical actions might not indicate a problem for the person diagnosed. And in any case of psychological suffering, general epistemic assumptions about how "language" operates separately from "minds," for instance, or "self" from "others," unavoidably condition the respective processes through which psychological processes: (a) develop, (b) are diagnosed, and (c) are intervened upon. This not only renders such assumptions unavoidable elements of any mental health program but points to broader sociohistorical planes of reference that care providers and service users share despite differences in narrative and values that often separate them.

By the mid-1970s, Bateson had started focusing much more explicitly on global ecological issues, applying his method of second-order cybernetics to topics like ecological aesthetics (Harries-Jones, 2008). At a time when Darwinian natural selection was the overarching framework for physical change, Bateson offered a new account that could account for wide-scale and often non-linear social effects of industrialization, like climate change. He connected this directly to mental health insofar as all mental processes at the individual level are part and parcel of broader social ecologies. As Chaney (2017) explains, Bateson's concept of the psychosocial double-bind was modeled on the idea of runaway processing paradoxes in computation that he learned at the Macy Conferences. With second-order cybernetics, Bateson reimagined capitalism in general as just such as a runaway system insofar as participants are forced to interact through inherently paradoxical patterns of social organization.[6]

At the same time, second-order cybernetics is not without criticism. The work of Bateson, Mead, and others have been described as harboring unrealistic optimism regarding the potential of cybernetics to shape global politics in ways other than through the military (Tiqqun, 2010). Deleuze and Guattari (2009) illustrate this, noting some of the contradictions in Bateson's personal journey:

> Gregory Bateson begins by fleeing the civilized world, by becoming an ethnologist and following the primitive codes and the savage flows; then he turns in the direction of flows that are more and more decoded, those of schizophrenia, from which he extracts an interesting psychoanalytic theory; then, still in search of a beyond, of another wall to break through, he turns to dolphins, to the language of dolphins, to flows that are even stranger and more deterritorialized. But where does the dolphin flux end, if not with the basic research projects of the American army, which brings us back to preparations for war and to the absorption of surplus value. (p. 238)

In one of the most comprehensive accounts of the cybernetic movement, Steven Joshua Heims (1991) explains how the Macy Conferences—and the cybernetics movement, more generally—were funded at least partially through Central Intelligence Agency initiatives to develop more effective forms of psychosocial intervention. It is easy to understand how such organizations would benefit from a method that can turn the world into a "trivial machine." Much of this was, moreover, under the guise of "mental health." Heims (1991), for instance, links Macy conference participants like Margaret Mead and Lawrence Frank to the development, in 1948, of the World Federation of Mental Health (WFMH). The organization's stated vision of "mental health [was] to help men to live with their fellows in one world," with "[t]he concept of mental health [considered] co-extensive with world order and the world community that must be developed so that men can live together in peace with each other" (c.f., Heims, 1991, p. 170). The explicit emphasis on goals like peace and world community, however, obscures the extent to which worldwide social order, at any cost, was the overarching goal of the WFMH. As Heims (1991) describes:

> The primary, and seething, mental health issue for so much of the world was to find autonomy from Western hegemony. Such men as

Mohandas Gandhi and the psychiatrist Frantz Fanon had appraised the psychological needs in non-Western countries far more reliably than had the organizers of the World Federation for Mental Health [WFMH]. The impetus for change had to come from below, and for many Africans and Asians it required opposing such Anglo-American plans for them as the WFMH. (p. 176)

Given the recently released documents regarding the CIA's ties to mind control experiments around the same time as the Macy conferences (see Bradley, 1984), there are reasons to remain critical about the links between the three organizations.

Today, the legacy of the WFMH is embodied in contemporary global mental health movements, including those forwarded by the World Health Organization (WHO), which some have criticized as extensions of earlier projects of Western imperialism (see Mills, 2014; Karter & Kamens, 2019; Dhar, 2019). As these critiques underscore, the assumption that psychosocial suffering is best understood, much less intervened upon, as if it were a global problem has been at the foundation of some of the most unethical applications of science throughout history. Some of these issues are outlined in more detail within Chapters 4 and 5 of this book. Insofar as concepts in psy-disciplines have steadily become translated into problems of control, information feedback, and data-collection, with interventions tending to be as systemic as possible, cybernetics has played an essential role in its historical development. And yet, when it comes to thinking about alternatives to the globalization of mental health services, particularly in their more standardized forms, the philosophy of technology developed by Gilbert Simondon, outlined next section, underlines some of the potentially useful aspects of cybernetics while, nonetheless, providing a critical assessment the baggage that has become associated with its overzealous social applications.

Gilbert Simondon and the role of affective modulation in transindividual networks

Gilbert Simondon's body of research represents a clear precursor to current critiques of cybernetics and psychosocial engineering. Especially relevant to the concerns of the current book, moreover, Simondon's career began just as the official Macy Conferences were tapering off. This positioned him uniquely to assess cybernetics from the outside the movement—and beyond the influence of the CIA—while nonetheless being part of the same socio-historical milieu from which it emerged. With English translations of his primary texts gradually becoming more widely available, there has also been growing interest in his work of late on the part of media theorists and philosophers. Given the broad acclaim Simondon received from many famous contemporaries (see Deleuze, 2004), it is surprising this has taken so long.

In contrast with cybernetic theorists like Wiener and Bateson, Simondon was not so much interested in topics like communication, self-regulation, and control. Working under the title of psychologist, he established a laboratory of general psychology and technology at Paris University V in 1963. This remained active for the next 20 years, and it is where he carried out most of his research. His version of experimental psychology, however, was much different than what most American psychologists were doing at the time—and still are today. Simondon approached issues like emotions, subjectivity, and experience as much as a physicist and a historian as a psychologist, seeking careful descriptions of the sociomaterial processes through which individuals and groups co-emerge. Simondon used the term *information* to describe such processes, insofar as this co-emerging always occurs in-the-form of constellations of affect, cultural artifacts, and thought. As he explains, "[i]nformation is not homogeneous with respect to its current structure, and there therefore remains in the individual a margin between the current structure and acquired information" (2007, p. 273). Simondon's theory of information can thus be distinguished from others based on his emphasis on two key qualities: (a) interoperability, where different types of information necessarily converge on each other; and (b) indeterminacy, where information is never structured in a static state (see Iliadis, 2013).

This is not, as such, the type of information based on one mind sending or receiving signals in relation to another; information simply *is* the technical process through which pre-individual fields composed of affect and sensation are integrated into networks that extend beyond individuals themselves. In this sense, Simondon's theory of technics—as a certain phase of human thought and action—is thus a direct function of his general psychology. Yuk Hui (2015) suggests that to fully appreciate the uniqueness of Simondon's concept of information:

> it is necessary to understand [individual] beings in terms of relations instead of substance. We can understand modulation as a constant becoming according to certain measures and constraints. Once being is understood in terms of relations, then being can be imagined as an

amplification in which different relations are modulated according to respective causes and effects. (p. 80)

The ongoing rearrangement (i.e., modulation) of such relations amounts to nothing less than the genesis of life *per se*—providing a unique approach to psychosocial ontogenesis, where each individual body is understood according to its unique capacities to form relations and experience affect with other bodies and objects. Modulation, in this sense, is a very specific form of control that, rather than being imposed on matter from the outside (as with hylomorphism), emerges through "internal tensions within any given being" (p. 77)—or what Simondon referred to as *disparation*. Hui further underscores how, for Simondon, links in thought (e.g., cause and effect) correspond not only to links across a series of physical elements, as with Descartes' mechanism, or even non-linear processes of cognitive feedback, as with cybernetics, but to highly complex sociomaterial and affective intra-actions[7] traversing otherwise discrete dimensions or phases of life. Such relations, moreover, are *intensive* rather than *extensive* in nature, given how they involve differences based on degrees of amplification or variation as opposed to categorical type.

Taking the manufacture of cars, for example, Simondon explains how they must be "conceived not only as a network [i.e., industrial] reality—like trucks—but as a social object, an item of clothing in which the user presents himself… [through] scale-like ornaments of psychosocial life—here they become paint, chrome, arials," etc. (Simondon, 2013, p. 11). With the design of cars, technical thinking and aesthetic imagination become fused culturally through processes shaped by both ergodynamics and fashion—encompassing the perception, sensation, and desires of individual users. The ways that affects within and beyond individual are modulated through the use and manufacture of existing technologies are thus positioned in a determining role for how new technologies are created. There can thus be no human culture or social life apart from contemporaneous technologies for the same reasons there can be no purely technical thinking without the sociocultural milieus that assign value to the affects produced through technological innovation itself.

Simondon's theory of information effectively elucidates the irreducible links between material tools, modes of feeling, and the technical styles of thinking that any person can inhabit at a certain time and place. As for cybernetics—as an intellectual and political movement—Simondon (2017) suggests it "can only acquire a universal sense in a society that is already constituted in a manner that conforms to this thought" (p. 148). In this sense, it is an embodiment of a special historical phase of human thought and organization—the explicit manifestation of an already emerging trend whereby discussions about cultural problems, dreams, desires, and creation myths merged into the production of technical objects, transforming material environments, living beings, and the relations experienced between them. This is how, for instance, "[t]ypes of machines are easily matched with each type of society—not that machines are determining, but because they express those social forms capable of generating them and using them" (Deleuze, 1992, p. 6). The cybernetic language Wiener sought to create could, as such, only become universal to the extent that contemporaneous sociocultural (and hence economic) conditions were able to support such a framework.

For Simondon (2017), cybernetics takes on additional value in cultural milieus where technologies can communicate directly with each other, as with current information networks. In this way, cybernetic technologies operate:

> *via* the mediation of already established channels of information, such as the exchanges, for example, between technics working synergistically on a given point…it is this type of grouping that Norbert Wiener cites as the source of this new technology, which is a technics of technics, at the beginning of his Cybernetics, published in 1948 and which is a new Discourse on Method, written by a mathematician teaching at an institute of technology. (p. 148)

While Simondon was undoubtedly influenced by cybernetics, the above excerpt similarly underscores his core critique of the movement. Specifically, he notes a tendency for Wiener and others to assume a privileged position in human history for digital technology while, at the same time, drawing arbitrary boundaries between human and non-human systems according to conventional philosophical assumptions about the individual. Cybernetics has thus uncritically "accepted as its point of departure that which [theories of] technology must reject: a classification of technical objects according to criteria established according to genera and species" (p. 60). Like Bateson, Simondon diagnosed a bias in Western thought to privilege certain concepts of *the individual* without accounting for the concrete conditions through which individuals and ideas (or information) about them emerge together. And yet, instead of repurposing cybernetics to intervene on habits of Western thought, as Bateson did, Simondon developed a reconstructive, psychosocial theory of technology through which history could be reimagined as a series of cultural concerns that earlier iterations of tools were tailored to address.

Simondon (2013) distinguishes his theory of technology from others throughout the history of Western philosophy, and by extension psychology, on the bases of two general principles. On the one hand, he links the creation of concepts to highly technical thought processes that extend beyond the concerns of any given philosopher. The ideas of individual theorists are, for instance, always conditioned by particular social institutions, government interests, and broader cultural forces. Theories are also shaped through the ways they are applied to create technical objects that serve these special interests. At the same time, concepts and objects produced with the aid of theory are not permanently wedded to certain cultural contexts, and for this reason, Simondon (2013) proposes that "*The subsets* [of a given technology] *are relatively detachable from the whole of which they are a part*" (p. 3, emphasis in original). There is thus no static essence of any particular technology precisely because it can always be granted a new set of values and uses within a different system of social affordances.

On the other hand, theoretical concepts are often refined in relation cultural problems that emerge through the use of those same tools. Technologies, theories, culture, and data participate in a range of socially iterative processes that necessarily exceed what we can say definitively about any one of them on their own.[8] Insofar as thought processes of individuals (especially academics) are always embedded within complex social relations—plugging both them and the tools they use into systems of social value at varying scales of cultural life—concepts must be understood at least partly in terms of the capacities for affect and sensation they modulate in relation to contemporary tools and mediums for social action. On this basis, Simondon (2013) provides a second principle for his theory of technology, grounded in regimes of functionality: "*if one wants to understand a being completely, one must study it by considering it in its entelechy, and not in its inactivity or its static state*" (p. 4, emphasis in original). The function of a technology, as such, can only be determined based on how it is used within processes of collective becoming that transcend individual persons themselves and are never fully complete.

Rather than talk about the ontology of being, as many Western philosophers have throughout time, Simondon was much more interested in processes of ontogenesis and the way individual bodies differentiate from each other though participation in shared activities. This presupposes a notion of pre-individual fields that moves beyond Freud's emphasis on early childhood relations—as determinants of personality—or the way DNA provides certain "building blocks" for life.[9] For Simondon, otherwise distinct dimensions of subjectivity, ranging from the technical and conceptual to the cultural, can only be understood in terms of how they emerge in complementary roles within singular moments of individuation. Through such processes of ontogenesis, disparate material elements and motivating forces come to form reticular relations through what he describes as *metastable* states. While such networks do not determine entirely how human development occurs, they nonetheless present a capacity for *transduction*, where individuals transition from periods of solitude into assemblages of complex *transindividual* relations that afford new opportunities for expressing individuality, as such.

Otherwise distinct objects or tools participate together in such processes in ways that accord with their respective functions and forms. Considering that each tool depends on earlier iterations of itself, as well as contemporary cultural problems, to be constructed in one form or another, each technology contains virtually within its current form all earlier versions of itself in addition to potential adaptations to social problems yet encountered. In this sense, each tool's existence literally *informs* how subsequent versions of it are created, while likewise possessing certain capacities unique to itself that can be amplified and reconfigured when used in concert with other tools through processes of social practice. Modulations of information thus correspond directly with amplifications or inhibitions of affective intensity. This is also what he would consider a process of individuation. For discrete elements to be perceived as separate from one another within a certain phase of metastability, signals must be continuously transmitted between them in ways afford realizations of their interconnections at various points throughout the process. There are no already constituted individuals—only pre-individual fields, processes of individuation, and transindividual networks.

By moving beyond childhood and transcending nuclear family relations, Simondon's concept of transindividuation serves as both an extension and a critique of the Freudian model of group psychology, with its foundation in the Oedipal myth (see Freud, 1921). Upon the birth of a newborn, for instance, the identities of both mother and father are radically transformed, but so are those of brother, sister, and aunt, through the evolving network of care revolving around the emergent (yet still nascent) human life. Each of these members of the family likewise go through respective material transformations as the child is languaged into its own individual development as part of the family. In this way, the nuclear family is not a self-contained unit divorced from relations beyond itself. Especially today, with information technologies broadcasting an increasing array of channels into each person's life, transindividual networks have a capacity to evolve in ways that Oedipal interpretations of child development simply cannot account for. And because they are continually evolving through systems of affect, which are not able to be fully observed, it is not even possible for such networks to be mapped or otherwise represented in their entirety.

Another reason that Simondon's concept of transindividuation is important to the concerns of the current book is because of what it implies about distinctions between the artificial and the natural. As he explains:

> Artificiality is not a characteristic that denotes the manufactured origin of the object as opposed to nature's productive spontaneity... A plant that has been made artificial can only exist in that plant laboratory, the greenhouse, with its complex system of thermic and hydraulic regulations. The initially coherent system of biological functions has been opened up to functions that are independent of each other and that are related to one another only by the gardener's care. Flowering becomes pure flowering, something detached and anoraic; the plant blooms until it is worn out and it produces no seeds. It loses its original abilities to resist cold, drought and solar heat. (Simondon, 2017, p. 49)

As opposed to comparing "human intelligence" to "machine intelligence," as if the former is somehow inherently more natural than the latter, both intelligence and artificiality can be understood in terms of the habits formed between proximal systems and the information exchanged between them. What counts as "natural" intelligence in one arrangement might be considered more "artificial" in another, while in others still it might not even count as intelligence at all. What is important here is not whether the materials of a system are either "man-made" or found in their current form outside of human society, which would merely posit an arbitrary boundary between humans and the rest of nature; rather, an artificial intelligence emerges when the very survival of a system has become entirely dependent on a specific set of arrangements, or control protocols, with other systems. Technologies in general are not inherently artificial, in this sense, as they each have a respective evolutionary logic that renders them more or less suited to particular ecological niches. And yet, they can become artificial insofar as the immanent logic linking their creation to their operation is superseded by forces outside of its otherwise natural ecologies. This is especially the case for those situated with broader artificial systems, like capitalism, for instance, where the abstract values of bodies and tools are regulated by protocols divorced from the psychosocial milieus out of which they individuate.

Throughout the history of psychology, topics like individuality, intelligence, and nature have remained central concerns for psychologists and psychotherapists. This is evident in: (a) Freud's attempts to use psychoanalysis as an intervention on personality development; (b) how behaviorists created artificial laboratory environments; and (c) the ways cognitive neuroscientists map information networks that they claim represent cognitive capacities in individual brains. Especially within the latter of these three, the concept of artificial intelligence (AI) has become a symbol with far-reaching social and psychological implications. Beyond its application to robotics and machine-learning, AI can likewise be understood as a metaphor for any attempt to program certain actions into a system by *controlling* for all other options. As I argue below, this can be true even in systems that might otherwise be considered natural, like organisms. The next chapter thus traces a critical history of the three psychological approaches noted above, exploring how they operate as social technologies that have been used to program individual behaviors through the construction of artificial conditions, as such. This history underscores important connections between Deleuze's (1992) concept of *societies of control* and Simondon's concept of *individuation*, insofar as the former afford a particular type of modulation that reinforces individuation in forms most conducive to the maintenance of transnational markets of capitalism. These overlaps are outlined in more detail in Chapters 4 and 5 of this book.

Notes

1 Significant portions of this chapter were taken from an earlier publication (Beck, 2020) with permission granted from its publisher, the APA.
2 According to Kline (2015), through Fremont-Smith's connection with the CIA, funds from its now famous MKULTRA project on the long-term effects of LSD and its relationship to mind control were redirected into several Macy Conferences, some of which specifically addressed the use of psychedelics.
3 Negative feedback refers to the capacity in a system to continually self-correct behavior by comparing a present state to a goal state.
4 During World War II, both Norbert Wiener and B.F. Skinner worked on parallel research projects for the US military. While Wiener worked together with engineer Julian Bigelow to develop his Anti-Aircraft Predictor (AA-Predictor), a machine that was supposed to anticipate the trajectory of enemy planes, Skinner was trying to develop a pigeon-guided missile (Pinto, 2014).

5 At the beginning of the 1949 Macy conference, key organizer Frank Fremont-Smith described this situation as such:

> The psychologists are pushed, as all of us are, by the impulses which comes from group feeling, and one of the things we need to know about is group feeling. One of the things we have right here is group feeling, group tension, and I hope some resolution and communication will take place. To some extent, we can be conscious of the dynamics of our own group relations...the [Macy] Foundation is interested not only in advancing a particular subject, whether it be the liver or feedback mechanisms, but also in setting a frame of reference in which communication across disciplines can take place. (Pias, 2016, p. 30)

6 In his collection of essays, *Steps to an Ecology of Mind*, Bateson (1987) states:

> A peculiar sociological phenomenon has arisen in the last one hundred years which perhaps threatens to isolate conscious purpose from many corrective processes which might come out of less conscious parts of the mind. The social scene is nowadays characterized by the existence of a large number of self-maximizing entities which, in law, have something like the status of "persons"—trusts, companies, political parties, unions, commercial and financial agencies, nations, and the like. In biological fact, these entities are precisely not persons and are not even aggregates of whole persons. They are aggregates of parts of persons. When Mr. Smith enters the board room of his company, he is expected to limit his thinking narrowly to the specific purposes of the company or to those of that part of the company which he 'represents.' Mercifully it is not entirely possible for him to do this and some company decisions are influenced by considerations which spring from wider and wider parts of the mind. But ideally, Mr. Smith is expected to act as a pure, uncorrected consciousness—a dehumanized creature.

7 Intra-action is a concept proposed by Karen Barad (2007) as an alternative to the notion of "interaction," given how interaction typically refers to relations between already established individuals while intra-action speaks to the way individuals emerge via their relations with each other.

8 The application of computer simulations to collect data informing climate science and policy is an excellent example of this. Experiments can now be carried out on imagined situations that have not yet occurred in order to collect data that might convince groups of people to "modify future behavior for the sake of *avoiding* an event" (Pias, 2016, p. 25). What is noteworthy here is not simply that data can ostensibly be collected about events that have not yet occurred, but that human action could very well be influenced on this basis of this data such that said events do not come to pass. This peculiar form of non-linear informational causality not only changes how temporal processes are understood in science but irrevocably alters the mechanisms by which science intervenes on human affairs in other social domains. It is thus worth noting how here computer simulation has fundamentally transformed the epistemological underpinnings of science in general.

9 Epigenetics has brought these fields of research together in ways that use a cybernetic framework to loop epigenesis, neural plasticity, and individual development in ways considered fundamental to life as we know it. (see, for example, Jablonka & Lamb, 2005).

3
THREE (PSYCHO)LOGICAL MYTHS OF AUTO-INDIVIDUATION (PSEUDO-AI)

Introduction

Psychology is, and always has been, a disordered discipline. At the turn of the 20th century, largely unrelated research programs across different parts of the world were carrying out experiments under "psychology" despite each group attending to notably different social concerns. As Edna Heidbreder (1939) describes in her book, *Seven Psychologies*:

> It is something of a paradox that systems of psychology flourish as they do on American soil. Psychology, especially in the United States, has risked everything on being a science; and science on principle refrains from speculation that is not permeated and stabilized by fact. Yet there is not enough fact in the whole science of psychology to make a single solid system. (p. 3)

Heidbreder forwards the concept of discrete "systems of psychology" to make sense of the divergent theoretical frameworks, and corresponding implicit assumptions, that developed across different universities at the time. As such, there are both historical and practical reasons to think about conceptual frameworks in psychology in terms of complex, cybernetic systems.

It is also relevant to note that the individuals who created early systems of psychology were trained under the norms of different disciplines, and thus the assumptions of different cultures. Freud, whose ideas are much more closely related to psychology than he was, was trained as a medical professional under clinicians like Josef Breuer and Jean-Martin Charcot. Wilhelm Wundt, who is widely credited with starting the first psychology laboratory, studied under experimental physicists like Von Helmholtz and Gustav Fechner. John Watson, the founder of behaviorism, studied under social philosophers and educators, including John Dewey, James Rowland Angell, and others associated with the functionalist school of social theory at the University of Chicago. Given the geographical and intellectual diversity of the contexts out of which these ideas emerged, such "schools of thought" were as much cultural ecosystems—networks of assumptions and preferences for certain tools—as conceptual frameworks.

One of the primary differences between systems of psychology is the units of analysis they focus on (e.g., defense mechanisms, structures of consciousness, stimulus–response pairs, etc.). As Bernard Scott (2016) explains, it has always been common practice in psychology to begin with elementary building blocks, ranging from "habits," "expectations," "stimulus–response bonds," to "memory states," "drives," "thoughts," "instincts," "cognitive processes," and "feelings" (p. 507). What is often assumed to bring them all together is their capacity to highlight something important about *the individual*. And yet, each theoretical system presupposes a different set of elementary units to describe what "the individual" means within it. Moreover, it has never been enough for psychologists to simply study individuals. The goal has always been to develop methods that can reliably intervene on individuals' emotions, thoughts, and/or behaviors, with the particular ways in which behaviors are shaped having always been conditioned by historically situated social values. In this way, much of the history of psychology can be defined according to a search for the proper unit of analysis to engineer intelligence, whether this be in the form of more conscious egos, appropriately shaped behaviors, faster brains, or smarter machines.

Any time a psychologist constructs an "artificially controlled" environment to produce knowledge, as such, its organization will unavoidably be conditioned by goals, assumptions, and technologies particular to a certain sociohistorical context. Such theory/context groupings are, in fact, what constitute the psychosocial systems described above, and likewise what constitutes the practice of experimental control. Here, mock situations are created that reduce a phenomenon to its most basic parts. There has always been a certain mytho-theoretical quality to such pursuits, whereby processes across irreducibly complex systems are truncated to fit within already available narratives of value and schemas of thought. In cybernetic terms, each systemic frame sets certain constraints—providing a general point of reference—under which high degrees of uncertainty (i.e., noise) observed in uncontrolled environments can be reduced to a predetermined target of individual variability. In the context of research, such frames of reference can operate consistently only insofar as they increase perceived order across persons (or brains) and situations they might encounter in life. Insofar as there are different aims and theoretical assumptions underlying each system or sub-discipline of psychology, there are also respective implications for what it means to be an *individual* under each systemic frame.

Through these various frames of reference, individual behaviors or thoughts are modulated along with the concepts used to intervene on them. Building on Simondon's insights about general psychology, this is the sense in which individuals become individualized through not only the conditions of their environments, but the thoughts and feelings other individuals experience in relation to them. While concepts of "the individual" tend to remain conceptually distinct from the material development of individual bodies, through processes of transindividuation they become incorporated into collective constellations of thought and affect (i.e., information). Such processes transcend any binary between thought and extension, as such. At the same time, the use of concepts in psychology presupposes certain pre-individual fields that condition what researchers can express with them and make them appear more useful for certain social purposes than others. In this way, the history of psychology outlined below does not analyze systems in psychology based on which ones are most *true*; rather, different systems in psychology are explored on the basis of what they are intended to *do*, as well as what needs to be presupposed to facilitate this social action.

In addition to the way cybernetics can be understood as a historical predecessor to current theories in cognitive science, this chapter explores how it can be applied as a theoretical paradigm for doing historical research in psychology. Here, I illustrate how and why the cybernetic movement of the 20th century is a necessary point of departure in making sense of the link between social order and psychological research. This has happened largely by refining the concept of control through theories and research about human motivation. Drawing on what is discussed in the introduction, this is aided by cybernetic metaphors, on the one hand, and new technologies available to psychologists, on the other. Together, these allow psychologists to reframe classic philosophical questions through contemporary concerns about technology, social norms, and world affairs.

Specifically, this chapter traces a critical history of psychological concepts of the individual through three *myths of auto-individuation*: (1) the individual psyche, (2) the individual organism, and (3) the individual brain. It is argued that, despite often being described in terms of self-organizing principles, each of these three concepts requires the creation of artificial, or in some sense highly controlled, systemic frames. Each one is likewise packaged with a particular set of assumptions and situated within broader narratives that are not insular to the discipline of psychology. There is thus a logical coherence in each of these myths insofar it corresponds to its own set of terms, technologies, social contexts, and historical problematics that it was created to solve. When all components of the myth are present, it functions. When too many component parts are missing, the myth fails to produce useful information.

In this sense, an historical drive towards scientism in psychology has also led to an increasingly digitized set of concepts—each one in turn depending on a highly controlled set of empirical conditions, as well as certain sociocultural values for its justification. For researchers to study individual psychology in ways that might perceived by others to be an *objective* manner, unaccounted-for effects of the ways certain boundaries are drawn between individuals and social contexts must remain implicit in how concepts of *the individual* have been defined. In other words, by ignoring the role of the observer (e.g., psychiatrist, psychologist) in how such first-order cybernetic systems are defined, psy-disciplines have continually perfected themselves as sciences, not of the human mind, *per se,* but of social control. The overarching goal: perfect mathematical algorithms that link the causes of human thought to future action.

Starting with Freud's approach to psychoanalysis, this chapter traces psychology's double movement of internalizing control into the individual while simultaneously externalizing the unconscious into the world, starting from early theories of human motivation—specifically the concept of *drive*. From psychoanalysis to behaviorism and cognitive neuroscience, the goal of researching human motivation has been to identify otherwise unobservable causes for human behavior in ways that allow for more effective interventions to be carried out under a prescribed set of conditions. For Freud, behaviors were *interpreted* as signs (i.e., symptoms) of the unique organization of an individual's psychic systems. Causes for behavior were situated largely within the individual unconscious, with analyst's task being to uncover how such causes maintain the boundaries of the analysand's broader psychic architecture. With behaviorism, on the other hand, causes for behavior became externalized into the immediate environment, despite remaining largely unconscious to the organism. For psychologists this allowed for a greater degree of precision in controlling the experimental conditions under which such causes are revealed. Finally, with cognitive neuroscience, maps of brain structures and neural networks have become tools used across disciplines and social contexts to decode hidden causes underpinning human behavior and recode them for increasingly varied social purposes.

Many of the current assumptions in cognitive neuroscience about how behaviors are conditioned in relation to environmental stimuli are based on principles of stimulus–response learning that developed out of operant conditioning. This is as true for schematic diagrams linking cognitive processes to external stimuli, often mediated through the brain, as it is for models of "reward circuits" linking the effects of certain neurotransmitters to social rewards for the person (or organism). While electrical circuits were used as a metaphor for the organism–environment field in behaviorist research, cognitive neuroscience has literalized this switchboard model by linking electrical activity inside the brain to perceptual and affective stimuli originating outside of it. Here, symbolic information processes operate in a sort of executive mediating function, discriminating between neurological processes that can be controlled from those than cannot.

Across all three general systems of thought, however, is an obvious trend whereby concepts of the unconscious have become progressively more visualized (and digitalized), yet also more abstract in relation to the situations out of which they developed. This, in turn, has allowed such concepts to become more easily linked to broader social narratives beyond psychology or psychiatry. In these ways, theories of human motivation have gradually been refined through new methods, technologies, and frames of reference emerging to solve different sets of sociohistorical problems. A change in focus from psychic processes to operant behaviors, for instance, and later to communication between neurons, entails different units of measurement, methods of data collection, and, by extension, conceptual schemas. This likewise brings different scales of observation (e.g., molecular, cognitive, socioeconomic) under the scope of *psychology*. Going even further, such methodological decisions can be situated within broader social narratives and values that connect respective units of analysis across different scales of reality to corresponding mediums of observation (e.g., the clinic, the laboratory, the office, the internet, etc.). Each mytho-theoretical framework described below thus entails a different logic of temporality and affords unique patterns of intervention on human behavior.

Psychoanalysis and the myth of psychic-individuation

Sigmund Freud's invention of psychoanalysis marked psychiatry's initial departure from asylums and hospitals in the 19th century, extending it into the lives of a much broader and more bourgeoise population of European citizens. This laid fundamental professional and conceptual groundwork for the full range of psychotherapeutic techniques that exist today—including the most common ones like Cognitive-Behavioral Therapy (CBT) and

Dialectical-Behavior Therapy (DBT). Despite Freud being one of the most controversial figures in the history of Western thought, many of his ideas (e.g., defense mechanisms, the importance of early childhood experiences) remain cornerstones of both theoretical and applied fields of contemporary psychology. And yet, the concept that Freud is perhaps most widely credited with creating, the unconscious, developed out of a substantial body of literature stretching at least to Friedrich Schelling (McGrath, 2011)—some would argue much farther. Rather than assume the unconscious is a universal construct, this section analyzes the function of Freud's psychoanalysis as a set of social technologies used to intervene on behaviors of analysands. Here, his concept of the unconscious operated as a guiding interpretive frame to be used under a circumscribed set of social situations (i.e., the psychoanalytic clinic).

Especially in relation to a discussion about cybernetics, however, there are other dimensions of Freud's work that merit the attention of contemporary psychologists, mental health professionals, and social theorists. Freud was a staunch advocate of the general utility of science, which accounts for his normative, psychosocial model of human health as self-organization. As Nigel Walker (1956) explains,

> Freud's use of the concept of homoeostasis, in the hypothesis that "the nervous system is an apparatus having the function of abolishing stimuli," is of great interest, not only because it represents the pessimistic core of his materialism but also because it appears to anticipate by a quarter of a century the notions of cybernetics. (p. 61)

The phrase "abolishing stimuli," above, refers essentially to the repression of individual emotions and sensations, which Freud took to be the primary mechanism each psyche uses to mediate between feedback from the environment and its innate drives. Determinations for which stimuli get abolished and which do not, while not made consciously, depend largely on how a person has learned to perceive themselves in relation to their world and interact with others up until that point. In addition to repression, there are various other defense mechanisms between consciousness and the world that protect the coherence of the psyche, as such. While this is clearly a mechanistic model of human thought, it is significantly more complex than Descartes' dualism. Given the way feedback between systems in the psyche can continually alter processes in each other, it bears more similarities to later notions in cybernetics (e.g., negative feedback, control, and circularity).

Overlaps between psychoanalysis and cybernetics are made especially clear in Freud's (1915) essay entitled, "The Unconscious." Here, Freud outlines an early vision for his metapsychology: a topographical framework whereby consciousness is described as one of several interacting subsystems within the broader psyche. In addition to the stream of thoughts and images that typically occupy our conscious attention, the essay outlines various unconscious drives that, being unable to become objects of consciousness themselves, can only be represented through ideas in ways that are heavily filtered through socially conditioned processes of censorship. Freud (1915) extolls the importance of this theoretical innovation, explaining that:

> [b]y accepting the existence of these (two or three) mental systems, psychoanalysis has departed a step further from the descriptive psychology of consciousness and has taken to itself a new problem and a new content. Up till now, it differed from academic (descriptive) psychology mainly by reason of its dynamic conception of mental processes; now we have to add that it professes to consider mental topography also, and to indicate in respect of any given mental operation within what system or between what systems it runs its course. (p. 123)

This effectively amounts to a method for mapping mental processes as dynamic, interacting sub-systems. To return to the issues of mental access introduced in chapter one, Freud's metapsychology offered a distinctly unique take on topic. On the one hand, Freud appears to have agreed with many contemporary psychologists that we can only infer the thoughts of others from "the utterances and actions we perceive [them] to make, and it is drawn in order that this behavior of [theirs] may become intelligible to us" (p. 120). On the other hand, he extended this condition to the access each person has to their own psychological experiences, going so far to say that "psychoanalysis demands nothing more than that we should apply this method of inference to ourselves," and that our own mental lives must be "judged as if they belonged to someone else and are to be explained by the mental life ascribed to that person" (p. 120).

If we take this last sentence seriously, it provides important insight into Freud's ontology and epistemology of mind. This is especially true when situated in relation to his understanding psychoanalysis, as an entirely new form of social praxis. Specifically, this bases psychoanalysis, and social interaction more generally, on the function of analogy in our interpretations of thoughts, emotions, and behaviors. By expanding upon such an inference-by-analogy model of *thinking about thinking* (i.e., metacognition) to include thoughts we have about ourselves, Freud further links thinking in general to symbolic mediation in a way that allows for multiple dimensions of thought be mapped within any given psyche. His model of the psyche thus integrates ideas of which we are to some extent conscious (immanent to Cs or Pcs), ideas we have repressed (immanent to Ucs), and affects (or drives) about which we are necessarily unconscious, into a single framework. Such modulations of the psyche act as reflections, or at times distortions, for one another. By learning how to read and intervene on such processes, Freud (1915) asserts the range of unconscious drives operating within a given psyche can come under the control of another (higher) order of mechanisms in ways that a person can become at least somewhat conscious of.

In Freud's later writings, he replaces this functional model of the psyche (conscious, preconscious, and unconscious) with a structural one, providing a new set of terms (ego, super-ego, and id) for the sub-systems of the psyche. With the latter, structural model, distinctions between consciousness and the unconscious are less clear-cut, as all three sub-systems refer to psychic processes with both conscious and unconscious aspects. A primary reason for this switch was clinical, as very few experiences described by analysands were ever purely conscious or unconscious. Psychoanalysis has always consisted of acts of tracing causes of psychosocial distress, and it would be meaningless to frame such symptoms as if they were entirely conscious or unconscious.

Freud's (1923) transition to a structural model allowed for individuation, as described above, to be mapped more precisely in terms of:

> a coherent organization of mental processes; and we call this his ego. It is to this ego that consciousness is attached; the ego controls the approaches to motility - that is, to the discharge of excitations into the external world; it is the mental agency which supervises all its own constituent processes, and which goes to sleep at night, though even then it exercises the censorship on dreams. (p. 8)

Despite the scientific validity of Freud's theories being commonly questioned by current psychologists, it is important to keep in mind that interpretations of unconscious processes were, for him, inextricable from psychoanalytic sessions with analysands. Here, "analysis is faced with the task of removing the resistances which the ego displays against concerning itself with the repressed" (p. 8). This reveals more explicitly than ever before a certain form of (psycho)logical mediation, as a series of psycho-affective defense mechanisms, as a core principle of psychiatric practice. The assumed psychosocial material expressed through such mechanisms "creates for itself, along paths over which the ego has no power, a substitutive representation (which forces itself upon the ego by way of a compromise)—the symptom" (Freud, 1924, p. 150, add Neurosis and psychosis). The task of the analyst is, as such, to read each analysand's unique psychic logic through interpretations of moments of transference, patterns of resistance, and mechanisms of repression, which are often exhibited through a series of symptoms, such that they can intervene according to their clinical training.

Transference is considered especially important to such processes insofar as it involves recognizing how the analyst is being perceived by the analysand and to what extent this can be symbolized and repurposed as a clinical intervention. With psychoanalysis, it is only by navigating between such highly coordinated trans- and intra-personal systems that the mechanisms underpinning the analysands' neuroticism can be properly deconstructed. Not only did Freud foreshadow the cybernetic model of homeostasis, therefore, he also considered the role of "the observer" to be an essential aspect of psychoanalytic practice. This is, again, why mediation—specifically between the analyst and analysand—was considered so important to psychoanalytic theory. His intention was for his theory to follow his practice.

At the same time, Freud did not follow through on this second-order insight enough to deconstruct his own presupposed mechanisms stemming largely from the sociohistorical context in which he found himself. Given how psychic processes of social censorship are always embedded within networks of social value, Freud's characterization of a healthy psyche as one that organizes itself should not simply be taken at face value. It is a direct reflection of the burgeoning emphasis on not only science and medicine as the authorial social practices but also the Enlightenment model of individuality. Freud's psychoanalysis was thus uniquely situated as a hinge between religious myth, Enlightenment values, and the emerging systems theories in the physical science. This is, in fact, what makes the concept of drive, and in turn myth, so important to his work. As he describes, "[t]he doctrine of drives is, so to speak, our mythology. Drives are mythical beings, spectacular in their indetermination" (Freud, 1933, p. 101). By setting up "a sharp distinction between the ego-instincts (= death-instincts) and the sexual instincts (= life-instincts)" (Freud, 1922, p. 19), Freud mythologizes the unconscious into a primal, unresolvable conflict between desire and dissolution of the self, which only a heroic journey through the unconscious can overcome.

Rather than use the term homeostasis to talk about how psychoanalysis intervenes on the interplay of such drives, Freud opts for the Oedipus myth as a normative model for psychosexual development. This is how he sutures the traditional interventions on psychic life, religion and myth, with the new ones, medicine and science. Nowhere are the implications of this for psychoanalysis laid out more clearly than his essay on *Group Psychology and the Analysis of the Ego*. Freud (1921) explains how "[a] little boy will exhibit a special interest in his father; he would like to grow like him and be like him, and take his place everywhere. We may say simply that he takes his father as his ideal" (p. 105). That is, until the boy grows up and kills the father, thus occupying the role of the hero in the myth. In contemporary life, of course, this takes on a symbolic dimension, which according to Freud becomes the primary lens for the ego when interacting with others in a group—or more specifically, between the ego and the ego-ideal.

The clinical act of psychoanalysis consists not in removing the lens of Oedipus entirely but in carefully substituting the right interventive symbols in a chain of symptoms such that the "normal" course of the psychosexual myth of development can pick up again wherever it left off. Here, the ego is interpreted as the mediator when and where reference is made to the "I." The analyst serves the role of the subject that is supposed to know what to do but, as Freud notes above, the drives themselves are unconscious, so the analysand inevitably supposes something about the analyst that even the analyst cannot have access to. Interventions on such mechanisms are thus enacted in the clinical relationship through an alternation of repetition and chance—coding and decoding the unconscious architecture of the analysand based on an abstract mythic structure that Freud believed applied to all humans.

To be sure, Freud was not simply adding new concepts to the body of psychiatric knowledge. The invention of psychoanalysis corresponds with the emergence of an entirely new logic of human speech and action and, with it, a corresponding set of social technologies. Such technologies, however, were revisions of older ones, and their use remained highly regulated by particular communities of analysts. This element of insularity within psychoanalytic practices is a popularly cited reason why they fell out of favor among American clinicians during the second half of the 20th century. Aaron T. Beck, the creator of cognitive-behavioral therapy, was one of the most vocal detractors, claiming that the communal relativism of psychoanalysis rendered it far too subjective—cultish, even. To become an analyst, the custom has always been for a person to go through analysis oneself. This has taken forms ranging from a formal series of analytic sessions to more informal group supervision meetings. This initiatory procedure is how analysts become endowed with the authority required to distinguish between socially normative behaviors and symptoms. To this day, however, the dividing line of psychiatric diagnosis serves as a mark of clinician's self-estimation as much as anything inherent to the person sitting across from them.

At the same time, the story of how psychoanalysis became such an influential force in America begins not with psychiatry but with public relations. It was Freud's nephew, Edward Bernays, who popularized psychoanalysis in America through his links with cultural leaders ranging from CEOs to politicians (Justman, 1994). As it turned out, the concept of the unconscious could be tailored to other social purposes, as well, even though its meaning was transformed in the process. Stripped of the interactive component it served in the context of clinical psychoanalysis, it became an empty container for all of American's hidden desires and wishes, which corporations then seized upon to sell more commodities. This provides an early example of psychological myths of auto-individuation being drastically altered through their circulation across institutions due to a perceived universal practical appeal that ignores the conditions out of which it developed, and the processes of individuation on which it intervenes.

Behaviorism and the myth of operant-individuation

There are at least two reasons the history of behaviorism is important to the aims of the current book. The first is simply the broad impact it has had on both psychology and psychotherapy in America. John Mills (2000) provides an excellent critical account of this in *Control: A History of Behaviorist Psychology*. He lays bare many of the theoretical and social assumptions underpinning behaviorism, connecting them to more general values in America at the time. Rather than being a-theoretical, as Skinner's research is sometimes characterized as (Moore, 2010), Mills underscores behaviorism's overarching theoretical commitments to positivism and pragmatism as guiding conceptual frames. Mills also exhibits how such assumptions and values were not purely academic; they were shaped by concerted attempts at social engineering and behavioral modification in ways that wedded universities to government interests and industry at the time. In perfecting John Watson's black box model of psychology, where unobservable states internal to the organism are disregarded, Skinner fulfilled

Watson's overarching mission to situate the most important causes of animal behavior in the environment. In this way, the concept of *control* was effectively able to be externalized beyond individual organisms, whereby their behavioral patterns could be mapped and conditioned according to the values of a growing range of social institutions.

The second reason the history of behaviorism is important to this book is because many ideas from Watson, Pavlov, Thorndike, Hull, and Skinner were reshaped into information frameworks across cybernetics and cognitive neuroscience (Cordeschi, 1991). Behaviorism and cybernetics likewise share a common goal of removing human exceptionalism from psychological theories of thought and action. However, rather than distancing itself from psychology by inventing a new social practice—like Freud did with psychoanalysis—behaviorists sought to transform psychology methodologically and conceptually into an empirical science of behavior modification that could be applied to pursuits ranging from marketing to education.

John Watson (1913) renders the full scope of such attempts clear in his behaviorist manifesto, asserting that:

> Psychology as the behaviorist views it is a purely objective experimental branch of natural science. Its theoretical goal is the prediction and control of behavior. Introspection forms no essential part of its methods, nor is the scientific value of its data dependent upon the readiness with which they lend themselves to interpretation in terms of consciousness. The behaviorist, in his efforts to get a unitary scheme of animal response, recognizes no dividing line between man and brute. The behavior of man, with all of its refinement and complexity, forms only a part of the behaviorist's total scheme of investigation. (p. 158)

From this theoretical foundation, boundaries conventionally assumed between organisms of different species were gradually reshaped, with all areas of human life translated into functional relationships between stimuli, responses, and reinforcement schedules between them. This presupposes that humans and other animals are largely ignorant of the causes of their own behavior and thus cannot be trusted as informants about their experiences. It is not that behaviorists ignore the unconscious completely, however, they simply externalize it into the environment and, in turn, code it in terms of functional relationships between drives and stimuli. In this way, behavioral reactions observed under experimental conditions are symbolized (i.e., encoded) as quantitative gauges that chart how such relationships should theoretically be expressed in other situations of a similar type.

In order to sustain a semblance of objectivity, the role of the researcher in ordering such symbols is reduced to the patterns through which mechanisms within the organism–environment system are modulated. This rests on a strict methodological empiricism, where any reference to phenomena that cannot be observed directly by researchers is restricted to only those most necessary for general laws of behavior conditioning to be exposed. Not entirely different from psychoanalytic theory, then, the truth value of behaviorist principles is determined by the extent to which they can be used to reliably intervene on behaviors under controlled conditions. While there are clearly proto-cybernetic elements to this approach (see Cordeschi, 1991), the linking of one behaviorist term to another in a chain of interventions similarly provides a concrete example of Descartes' mechanistic logic applied to human psychology. And yet, behaviorists are unique in that they attempt to account for the consciousness of the observer (i.e., researcher) by ignoring it not only in themselves, but also whatever organisms they happen to be observing.

Ivan Pavlov's famous studies on dogs provide excellent examples of this behaviorist logic at work. By surgically implanting salivation tubes on the faces of a group of dogs, Pavlov developed a method to measure changes in their reflexive responses such that they could be paired with controlled experimental conditions. This is often hailed as an important foundation for all succeeding quantitative approaches to behavioral research. And yet, what made Pavlov's research truly groundbreaking was not that he discovered universal principles of animal behavior—he did no such thing—but that he illustrated precisely how certain socio-affective dependencies can be conditioned in a specific group of experimental subjects. In other words, what is often left out of conventional accounts of Pavlov's research is: (a) his own role in interacting with his dogs, whom he was already quite familiar with (and vice versa); and (b) the general knowledge he must have had access to about dogs—to know, for example, that meat would elicit gastrointestinal effects in ways that could be linked to a new signification of Pavlov's own (subjective) choosing (i.e., a bell rather than something else).[1]

In this way, Pavlov, his dogs, and the technical apparatuses to which the subjects were attached formed a complex, cybernetic system, with feedback loops inhering between each of their actions and reactions that evolved across experimental trials. Extending the cybernetic lens even further, we can understand Pavlov, as "the experimenter" in this situation, as occupying the role of the second-order observer described last chapter. According to Pavlov's own methodological decisions, the experimental field of the dog–machine–environment system became structured by certain historical constraints—ranging from the technology available to what is known about physiology. The functional relations that Pavlov measured were not simply natural reactions to stimuli; such responses elicited in the dogs were dependent on Pavlov's own actions and mediated by the technology of the apparatus. Drawing on Simondon, furthermore, this might be understood as measures of technical modulation where the physiology of his dogs became dependent on a certain set of artificial arrangements.

Later behaviorist research in America built upon Pavlov's principles of classical conditioning by incorporating technology in similar ways. John Thorndike, for instance, studied behavioral change in cats by placing them in mechanical puzzle boxes, where they were confined alone until they pulled a loop freeing them and providing access to food. Through this research, Thorndike developed the notion of stimulus–response (S–R) bonds, later formalized into his *Law of Effect* (Thorndike, 1911). Essentially, this formula was used to quantify the probability an organism will select (i.e., discriminate) between different stimuli, which Thorndike believed to be learned over time through a series of interactions between an organism and its environment. Thorndike's concept of the S–R bond was formalized according to the following terms:

> The situation (S) evokes a variety of responses; one response (R) happens to be followed by satisfaction (S^R); the satisfier stamps in a connection or bond between the situation and the response; and as a result, when the same situation is presented, the response is more likely to occur. (Nevin, 1999, p. 447)

The term *satisfaction* above refers to the cessation of motivating factors immanent to the organism that become linked to a stimulus through the enaction of a certain behavior (i.e., a response). In this mechanistic model, the response is understood as the function or mechanism that reinforces the association between satisfaction and the stimulus. In this way, "the situation sets the occasion for responses to be followed by reinforcers, leading to an increase in response probability" (Nevin, 1999, p. 447). This makes it possible for the history of an organism, as such, to be encoded into a formula regarding how such an organism might behave under specified conditions in the future. It likewise allows for the situation to be reduced to a set of controlled variables. As more data is collected, the higher the probability of predictive capacity and, as such, the higher the possible degree of behavioral control. And yet, it is important to keep in mind that this encoding—of the situation as well as the history of the organism—occurs entirely from the perspective of the observer (i.e., the behaviorist researcher). This essentially occurs at a first-order cybernetic level that ignores the influence of not only culture and cognitive bias but also the role of the researchers and their machines that mediate each subject's relations with the environment to effectively speculate on its on-going development.

The general goal of developing a formula that can reliably predict and control the probability of future human behavior was elevated to new heights by neo-behaviorist Clarke Hull. Hull was critical of what he considered to be the overly subjective nature of most theories of behavior, including Thorndike's, and was likewise interested in the ways experimental conditions themselves set frames around observation and description within empirical research. At the same time, he considered some degree of speculation necessary for research on topics (like human behavior) that are inherently difficult to observe, noting how "in some cases there may be employed in scientific theory a whole series of hypothetical unobserved entities; such a series is presented by the hierarchy of postulated physical entities" (p. 21). He simply felt that such concepts should be restricted to those necessary to deduce general principles that link what has already been observed to a logical series of functions. He points to examples in physical sciences, for example, including "molecules supposedly being constituted by atoms and the atom in turn being constituted of electrons" and so on (p. 21), referring to such concepts as *intervening variables*—essentially placeholder terms that represent "entities or processes which, if existent, would account for certain events in the observable molar world" (p. 21).

For Hull (1943), in order to explain what happens between stimulus and response, it is necessary to posit a behavioral drive in the form of just such an intervening variable. He describes, for instance, how "the general concept of drive (D) tends strongly to have the systematic quality of an intervening variable or X, never directly observable" (p. 57). With this basic drive reduction theory, Hull seeks to avoid subjectivism in research on human drives by starting with "colorless movement and mere receptor impulses" and from there collecting quantitative data in ways that "build up step by step both adaptive behavior and maladaptive behavior" (p. 25). Through this strictly deductive approach, Hull (1943) creates a framework to translate behavioral responses, as parts of cycles, into symbols that mediate between unobservable drives internal to the organism and observed environmental stimuli. Building upon ideas from earlier behaviorists, specifically Thorndike's Law of Effect, Hull's drive reduction theory can be expressed in the following formula (see Jackson, 2010, pp. 58–59):

$$_sE_R = {_sH_R}(D)$$

where,

$_sE_R$ is excitatory potential (likelihood an organism produces a response (R) to stimulus (S))
$_sH_R$ is the habit strength (derived from previous conditioning trials)
D is drive strength (determined by, for example, the hours of deprivation of food)

It became more complex over time, however, with Hull gradually refining it into the following form:

$$_sE_R = V \times D \times K \times J \times {_sH_R} - I_R - {_sI_R} - {_sO_R} - {_sL_R}$$

where,

V is stimulus intensity dynamism (the degree of influence of the stimuli, e.g., light strength),
K is incentive (the appeal of the result of the action),
J is the incentive based on the delay of reinforcement,
I_R is reactive inhibition (inhibition caused by, e.g., fatigue),
$_sI_R$ is conditioned inhibition (inhibition caused by continual performance of a behavior that does not dissipate over time),
$_sL_R$ is Reaction threshold, the smallest amount of reinforcement that will produce learning,
$_sO_R$ is the momentary behavioral oscillation (error).

Hull characterized the above series of terms as functional mechanisms that, if properly controlled, observed, and measured, should allow future researchers to shape the behaviors of organisms in line with predetermined goals. The definitions of such terms were likewise influenced the general vision shared by Hull and others at the time of organisms as fundamentally self-organizing agents.[2] So long as the environment is optimally structured, according to this perspective, organisms should naturally alter their behaviors to reestablish a sense of homeostasis. Agency, as it were, is not an internal property of organisms themselves; it can only be conditioned into behavioral responses through the way stimuli are arranged form one environment to the next. Characterizing the organism as self-organizing system, as such, belies the way behaviorism effectively externalizes control over the organism's agency, as their behaviors become increasingly dependent on antecedent and surrounding conditions.

Under these experimental conditions, intervening variables enact frames of reference whereby data sets can be interpreted and integrated into broader programs of behavioral research and social control. Despite such terms working relatively well as operational variables under the experimental conditions imposed by Hull, they tended to break down, however, when applied outside of those settings. What this essentially reveals is Hull's conflation of a description of objective facts about a given organism/environment system with the results of intentional control on the part of the researcher. Guttman (1977) goes as far to refer to these terms as an "artificial chain of explanatory variables" that, despite no longer being useful for psychological purposes, represent an overarching behaviorist impulse to reduce human behavior to their most basic component parts, which can then be reprogrammed from the ground up (p. 321). Drawing on Simondon's notion of the artificial, this can be understood as an attempt to program specific behaviors to occur exclusively under an artificially delimited set of circumstances, determined by external forces arranged by a second-order observer.

Hull and Baernstein (1929), in fact, connect behaviorism to artificial intelligence explicitly, writing:

> If it were possible to construct non-living devises – perhaps even of inorganic materials – which would perform the essential functions of the conditioned reflex, we should be able to organize these units into systems which would show true trial and error learning with intelligent selection and the elimination of errors, as well as other behavior ordinarily classed as psychic. (pp. 14–15)

In these ways, Hull's series of intervening variables came to represent a growing social impulse to program artificial intelligence in machines much more than they did any universal principles of animal behavior. This also foreshadowed by half a century the data collection practices of current tech-companies, who use behavioral data to refine machine learning algorithms based on cybernetic feedback loops that, in turn, allow a greater variety of data to be collected on humans over time. Despite Hull's framework coming to be considered obsolete for psychological research, therefore, it nonetheless offers an excellent historical example of two phenomena with relevance to the current book: the limits of Descartes' mechanism and the behaviorists' pragmatic substitution of social control for empirical fact.

It was perhaps the most famous behaviorist, B.F. Skinner, who had the most radical vision of the organism–environment relationship. In Skinner's framework, behaviors are not simply expressions of the history of the individual but form complex links across all members of their own species. This is how otherwise automatic behaviors, or unconditioned responses, can be distinguished from learned action. As Skinner (1953) explains:

> In both operant conditioning and the evolutionary selection of behavioral characteristics, consequences alter future probability. Reflexes and other innate patterns of behavior evolve because they increase the chances of survival of the species. Operants grow strong because they are followed by important consequences in the life of the individual. (p. 90)

Each new behavior an organism learns is thus considered an *operant*, hence the term operant conditioning. Operants which prove most useful for the organism over time can be enacted more quickly in response to a greater variation of stimuli of a similar type. Skinner's approach to operant conditioning was, in this sense, developed precisely, albeit unwittingly, to research Simondon's concept of artificiality. Here, each experimental subject does not merely react to a stimulus, but is moreover conditioned to perceive its desired stimulus anywhere, otherwise it would be less likely to act according to general expectations. Skinner was thus as much a social engineer as a psychologist, constructing elaborate mechanical devices and chambers where pigeons could, for example, be taught to peck only at certain words or perform ritualized responses to be given food. Such machines could be programmed to interact with organisms in very precise ways, all the while collecting data that could be integrated into *reinforcement schedules*, which were used in turn to refine the technical components of the machine. Skinner would come to discover that the most useful reinforcement schedules are variable, unable to be predicted, and based primarily on positive reinforcement. In this way, highly desirable rewards that are consistently extended further and further beyond expectation prove to be more effective forms of punishment than any aversive stimuli ever could.

The sheer scale of Skinner's research transformed the notion of control from being merely a single aspect of experimental research to constituting the entire process. One example of this was the way he treated the rats he used as subjects, which were bred, starved, and isolated to control their reactions as much as possible. Under these conditions, discipline is not immediate but gradually modulated, deferred to a later date, and mediated through progressively more complex forms of technical conditioning, ranging from reinforcement to negative punishment. The drives of the organism become modulated according a series of alternations between delayed gratification and threat of discipline, essentially programming behavior through a continuously refined pattern of oscillating amplifications and contractions of key environmental stimuli. Skinner referred to these highly concerted systems of conditioning as schedules of reinforcement. Social applications of such a method became increasingly obvious to managers and executives across organizational settings, and Skinner was among the most explicit about the extent to which behaviorism should be used to engineer social behavior. He went so far, in fact, to refer to operant conditioning as a "technology of behavior" and even more specifically "technology of teaching" (Skinner, 1984), while pushing consistently for it to be applied to issues in psychiatry and psychotherapy (Guttman, 1977).

Through such highly technical, machine–organism systems created in his laboratories, Skinner developed paradigmatic cybernetic research devices, and yet, by ignoring the role of the researcher in how such systems were organized, such systems remained at a socially normative, first-order cybernetic level. By restricting himself to such a strict version of empiricism, moreover, where his terms were operationalized exclusively based on what could be observed within research settings, Skinner made it nearly impossible for behaviorism to account for complex human behaviors like language. Blind allegiance to his own vision of radical behaviorism, however, left him convinced otherwise, stating in 1957 that "the basic processes and relations which give verbal behavior its special characteristics are now fairly well understood," adding that "the results [of his animal research] have been surprisingly free of species restrictions" (1957, p. 3).

There is perhaps no greater example of the hubris of behaviorism than the previous quote. In seeking to translate the history of any given organism, and in some cases, species, into a series of empirical observations and intervening variables, the theories of behavior outlined above omit what is the most important motivator for any organism at all: social relations in the present moment. To reach the level of control necessary for behavioral responses in laborites to be quantitatively coded and turned into principles, individual organisms had to be removed from the social and material ecologies in which their bodies evolved to inhabit, then resituated into some of the most artificially crafted environments imaginable. Because of the simplicity of stimuli in these environments, and the way behaviorism externalizes agency in the form of adjacent stimuli, it is tempting to believe that any given stimuli can simply be reproduced *en masse*, effectively rendering it more efficient to alter the environment around individuals than to learn what they might be capable of under new circumstances.

But of course, behaviorism was always more than a set of academic theories. It developed out of broader American values, like pragmatism and technicity, and its methods have been continually refined to support them. If nothing else, behaviorism provides an excellent example of how a theoretical frame of reference (i.e., a myth of auto-individuation) can structure research decisions across settings, simply through assumptions and concepts exchanged through published research. In this way, Skinner programmed social norms into his organisms by modulating their affect in relation to artificially constructed environments. As more data was collected by behavioral researchers, the higher the probability of predictive capacity and, as such, the higher the possible degree of behavioral control. It is important to keep in mind, however, that this encoding—of the situation as well as the history of the organism—occurs entirely from the perspective of the observer (i.e., the behaviorist researcher). This remains at a first-order cybernetic level that ignores the influence of not only culture and cognitive bias but also the role of the machines mediating the organisms' relations with their environments.

In the end, Skinner's inability to account for complex human action, specifically language, would be the undoing of his radical behaviorism. In 1967, Noam Chomsky published what would end being one of the most cited essays ever in psychology—a critique of Skinner's research on "verbal behavior." Here, Chomsky (1967) argues that:

> Skinner's claim that all verbal behavior is acquired and maintained in "strength" through reinforcement is quite empty, because his notion of reinforcement has no clear content, functioning only as a cover term for any factor, detectable or not, related to acquisition or maintenance of verbal behavior. Skinner's use of the term conditioning suffers from a similar difficulty. Pavlovian and operant conditioning are processes about which psychologists have developed real understanding. Instruction of human beings is not. (p. 142)

According to Chomsky, it is impossible to translate all the most important factors that contribute to human language into the research vocabulary of behaviorism because language is not merely learned through associations made between basic stimuli and one's own behavioral reactions. For Chomsky, to understand the development of language it is necessary to account for certain capacities, likely innate, to process information in the form of syntax (i.e., grammar), and "what is necessary in such a case is research, not dogmatic and perfectly arbitrary claims, based on analogies to that small part of the experimental literature in which one happens to be interested" (p. 142).

Despite the many attempts by neobehaviorists, like Hull and Skinner, to make behaviorism as objective as possible, there have always been inherent limitations to what could be understood about human life through a strictly behaviorist framework. On one hand, Skinner's myth of operant-individuation, whereby all individual differences are reduced to a set of operants most strongly established in each organism's life, has proven to be useful in the broader pursuit for technologies of social engineering. Behaviorism provided society with an entirely new approach to human management that, while transforming Freud's mythic theory of drives, created itself in a highly technical form. The diagrams behaviorists construct from their research are based on principles of behavior that, despite being highly truncated representations of life, can be successfully replicated across social contexts of varying types; even if this often requires restructuring the environment in which behaviors occur to maintain a degree of control that would otherwise only be found in a laboratory.

At the same time, it is important to recognize the essential role interpretation serves in operant conditioning. Behaviorism, in general, externalizes the unconscious causes of behavior into the environment, but it ignores the role of the researcher in organizing that same environment. It is as if behaviorists somehow reach the conclusion that, because of the degree of objectivity it offers, it is in the long run more ethical, in fact, to exert more control over the behaviors of others than of oneself. Historically, however, this has clearly not been the case. Building on this insight, the next section explores how Skinner's myth of operant-individuation has been combined with innovations stemming from cybernetics and tailored to conduct research on the brain. Here, a new framework, cognitive neuroscience, emerges based on notions of the neuron as an all-or-nothing principle and the cerebral cortex as the principle site of control. Brain-imaging technologies and general maps of neural architecture have, as such, been perpetually reconfigured such that these two mechanisms can be conjoined into a single myth of auto-individuation.

Cognitive neuroscience and the myth of cerebral-individuation

This section brings the histories outlined so far full circle in two, overlapping ways: a return to mental processes, through a turn to cybernetics. During the 1950s, in the wake of the first digital computers, experimental psychologists in America began turning away from behaviorism as their preferred theoretical paradigm. This is commonly described as a return to the study of mental processes—a cognitive revolution. And yet, outside of behaviorists' strict refusal to theorize about anything other than observed action, the mind—in one form or another—has consistently been the primary focus for most psychologists around the world. As George A. Miller (2003), an early pioneer of cognitive psychology, explains:

> Whatever we call it, the cognitive counter-revolution in psychology brought the mind back into experimental psychology. I think it is important to remember that the mind had never disappeared from social or clinical psychology. It was only experimentalists in the US who really believed that behaviorism would work. (p. 142)

Miller (2003) goes on to account how early in his career he sought to reinterpret Skinner's operant conditioning through the mathematical theory of communication (MTC) developed by Claude Shannon (1971). Shannon, a Macy Conference attendee, developed one of the first frameworks linking information to communication, proposing that information is always encoded at the point of sending and decoded at the point of reception. This model was based on Markov probability chains in mathematics, where any given state of affairs is considered entirely dependent on the conditions immediately preceding it in continuous time. For Miller, this framework appeared compatible with Skinner's switchboard framework, where environmental stimuli and behavioral responses were linked together in a similarly continuous way. After a while, however, Miller gradually concluded that Chomsky's critique of behaviorism was so persuasive that any strictly statistical, empirical approach to the study of psychology would be too reductive. He and a group of colleagues at Harvard then built a research program around Jerome Bruner's social psychology, which gradually became its own paradigm, cognitive psychology, and steadily supplanted most behaviorist programs across American universities.

While this was going on in American psychology departments, researchers in other fields had begun studying the brain in ways that extended cybernetics in altogether different ways. While the official series of Macy Conferences began in 1946, they were preceded by a group of more informal meetings that started four years earlier. In May of 1942, Wiener, Lawrence Frank, Mead, Bateson, McCulloch, Mexican physiologist Arturo Rosenblueth, and psychiatrist Lawrence Kubie were brought together by Frank Fremont-Smith, the Macy point person, with Milton Erickson and Howard Liddell leading a discussion on hypnotism. The title of this gathering was simply the "Cerebral Inhibition Meeting," a direct reflection of the neuro-psychological orientation of the conversations. While the entire conference was considered a success, it was the presentation on overlaps between engineering and human behavior by Rosenblueth and Wiener that left attendees the most excited about these transdisciplinary meetings moving forward (Heims, 1991). Similar to Shannon's theory, the central theme of their presentation was that human behavior is inherently goal orientated and, even if goals change from one moment to the next, actions must be understood in terms of continuous feedback loops between the present and immediately preceding state. Taking this a step further than Shannon, however, they also proposed a model linking the inhibition of neuronal activity to behavioral processes through non-linear loops of communication between the two levels.

While this early notion of neuronal communication was used loosely by Rosenblueth and Wiener to explain information processes across brains, minds, and behavior, several attendees subsequently tailored it to their own research. In 1943, for instance, three years prior to the first official Macy Conference, two of Weiner's students, Warren McCulloch and Walter Pitts, published a paper on their now famous *McCulloch-Pitts model* of the neuron. This was one of the first studies to demonstrate mathematical implications of representations of the neuron in terms of an all-or-nothing (i.e., binary) principle. This, in turn, allowed neural impulses to be mapped as digital processes, or networks, with relations between points modeled on Boolean algebra (Abraham, 2002).

With the emergence of the first digital computers, the McCulloch-Pitts model of the neuron provided a new way to think about human behavior, as well as a new mathematical model to rethink computer processes as neural networks. This marks one of the first points in human history that the temporal processes underpinning brains and machines, respectively, could be mapped in the form of an analogous, mathematically ordered calculus. As the conceptual link between neurons and digital computers became progressively more stamped into the vernacular of various disciplines, the McCulloch-Pitts model emerged as a dominant approach to thinking about the human thought (Abraham, 2002). Packaged with all the assumptions that construing thought as a series of digital sequences entails, it has since, then, become something of a default approach to mapping neuronal activation in relation to brain states.[3]

It is no coincidence that this series conceptual developments overlapped historically with other innovations in tech that allowed brain activity to be mapped in real time. From phrenology and Golgi stains to lobotomies and lesion experiments, researchers have long sought to link rough sketches of the brain to behavioral functions. Prior to the 1950s, however, there were essentially only two methods available to observe the structure of brains in living people: X-ray and, in some cases, ultrasound (Rose & Abi-Rached, 2013). Electroencephalography (EEG) could yield measurements of electrical activity in the brain but not maps of a region or the organ itself. The development of CAT (computerized axial tomography) imaging offered researchers something notably different. For the first time ever, mathematical algorithms could be combined with computer programs "to assemble the results of repeated X-ray "slices" across the brain to produce an image of an anatomical slice, showing the internal structure to the extent that it was made up of tissues of different densities" (Rose & Abi-Rached, 2013, p. 68). This provided researchers with a non-invasive method to map structural images of brains and other parts of the body, revealing subtle variations between layers of tissue that would otherwise be nearly impossible to observe.

Other brain-imaging technologies, like Positron-emission tomography (PET) and functional magnetic resonance imaging (fMRI), have since been created that, rather than scanning the structure of a brain, can track its function—though each relies on a notably different set of techniques. PET, for instance, uses radioactive tracers within a certain range of isotopes, which can be coupled—through injection or ingestion—to target molecules already in the body, ranging from oxygen to cocaine (Dumit, 2004). Once inside, such tracers follow along with the linked molecule throughout its regular metabolic activity. As the tracer decays, it emits signals that are picked up by the PET—meaning that resulting "brain images" are, in fact, simulations of data based on metabolic processes related to whatever molecule the tracer happened to be attached to at a given moment in time. According to Joseph Dumit (2004), signals are sent from the radioactive material in bursts, so detecting them relies on closely related "coincidences" between desired signals over relatively short periods. If signals are spread out too far, or are not strong enough, there can be gaps (e.g., "noise") in the dataset that render them useless. In this sense, strong PET datasets rely on very precise coordination between (a) the timing of the isotope decay, (b) the rate of metabolic activity of the coupled molecule, and (c) the target area that the researchers hope to scan. With any given dataset, moreover, it is not clear exactly to what extent it represents what was actually going on in the target brain at the time.

Based on complex algorithms programmed into the computer software, datasets are produced in the form of a collection of 3-dimensional boxes, or "voxels," each containing a number that represents the state of the tracer at a certain point in time. Although simply producing a PET dataset is not enough for a brain image to be produced. The dataset must also be reconfigured into a form that can be mapped onto a second, anatomical dataset, typically "either the subject's own MRI, for instance, or a reference brainset...*a generalized human brain*" (Dumit, 2004, p. 81, emphasis in original). Reference *brainsets* are essentially amalgams of a series of MRIs on a group of controls, which serves as an *atlas*. There are several of such atlases in circulation across different labs, each one having certain advantages and disadvantages. Using one atlas over another is likely to have some noticeable effect on the algorithm read out, ultimately altering the final image in ways that are difficult to predict (Dumit, 2004).

If the researcher decides to collect MRI data for the study, there is a similarly lengthy process as there is with PET. This involves, first, emitting a magnetic field around the person that stabilizes protons throughout the body and, then, sending bursts of radio frequencies within a predetermined plane to perturb all the protons within that target area. Upon return to a resting state, the protons wobble, releasing energy that allows them to be contrasted with protons outside of the target plane, which remain held in place by the broader magnetic field projected at the outset of the imaging process. As Cohen et al. (1993) explain, this can detect signs of activity on various levels of specificity insofar as:

> Protons belonging to different types of molecules release energy at different frequencies as they recover, providing characteristic signatures for each molecular type. Standard MRI applications measure the energy released from protons in water, since this is the most abundant molecule in biological tissues and therefore provides the strongest signal. This signal is useful, since different tissues have different water contents. Differences in signal strength, therefore, can be used to generate high-resolution structural images.

MRI brainsets are thus useful here because they produce structural (anatomical) images of the brain that can fill in the gaps in the physiological dataset produced through PET. fMRI, by contrast, works by measuring the energy released from neurons after they fire. It can produce higher resolution physiological data than PET and does not require any radioactive isotopes. However, it is much more susceptible to "noise" resulting from subtle movements on the part of participants during data collection. Either way, once combined with MRI data, the quantitative voxels from physiological datasets can be given a relative anatomical location in "the brain." Finally, a three-dimensional map of what is supposed to be the original brain activity is produced.

What is most important to understand about this highly complex process is that each step indexes various possible techniques a researcher must select from, with each choice having certain tradeoffs in terms of the overall fidelity of one or another aspect of the final product (a single brain-image). Different labs commonly use different techniques, making it incredibly difficult for any set of maps generated from one study to be compared accurately with those from another one. Also, no brain imaging technology can map brain processes on its own, so multiple datasets are always needed to create the colorful scans scattered across many textbooks. And this does not yet account for the complexity underpinning the experimental procedures involved in conducting a full-scale study. Given how cognitive neuroscientists are generally interested in general structures and function of the human brain, too much individual variability is anathema to the cause. Two of the primary issues thus become: (a) how to, as much as possible, reduce "noise" (e.g., measurement error, to technical error, procedure error, too much participant movement, etc.) to produce useable data and (b) how to modulate aspects of the final image in a way that visualizes what the researchers want others to see (i.e., different regions of the brain are not naturally the colors we see in scans). This process is as much art as science.

Typically, when brain-imaging technologies are used for psychological research purposes, the goal is to correlate participant performance on a simple task with concurrent neural activity. The assumption is that this should allow researchers to determine a probability for whether certain areas of a brain will be activated during similar tasks on future occasions. This is essentially a rudimentary form of behaviorism coupled with PET and MRI. Much of the research conducted on brains over the last few decades have utilized a method referred to as the *logic of subtraction*, developed initially in the 1800s by Frans Donders (1869)—a student of

Wilhelm Wundt. Donders' method essentially involved a comparison of two sets of general research components: (a) a baseline measure of the time between a stimulus (S), also referred to as a signal, in the person's (P) environment and a reaction (R), or detectable movement; and (b) a measure of those same variables after the *insertion* of a mental process, or an elementary cognitive task (ECT), into the situation by the experimenter (E). By subtracting the first set of measures from the second, the idea is that the difference in time represents the amount of time required to carry out that task. Donders obviously did not have access to currently existing brain-imaging technology, so any links he imagined between behaviors and neural processes were largely speculative. But analogous subtraction methods are used today by comparing different brainsets under similarly controlled conditions to determine which areas of "the brain" were activated in an ECT group as opposed to the control group.

Together, these experimental technologies and research procedures constitute the primary toolset that cognitive neuroscientists use to study human behavior and, ostensibly, thoughts and emotion. In an almost identical fashion as behaviorism, cognitive neuroscientists operationalize variables based exclusively on what can be observed in an experimental setting. With the range of digital technologies at their disposal, the assumption is that their procedures can render a much wider range of variables visible for measurement. However, measurement is mediated through a repertoire of digital technologies and neural maps. For a series of neurological effects to be translated into cognitive processes, as such, they must be logically reconstructed through statistical correlations between PET data gathered from metabolic processes on an individual, a second brainset or atlas, stimuli in the person's environment, and their measured behavioral reactions—all while keeping any "noise" within each respective domain to a minimum. This is precisely the idea of a first-order cybernetic system Wiener envisioned for brain research. As Uljana Feest (2012) describes, this is also a prime example of how "scientific theorizing, especially in neuroscience and the biological sciences... proceeds by way of constructing models of mechanisms, where mechanisms are conceived of as entities and activities organized such as to realize (exhibit or cause) instances of a phenomenon of interest" (p. 179). And yet, it is important to keep in mind that brain-imaging research is nowhere near precise enough to determine temporal precedence to the extent that causal relationships can be confirmed with certainty. At best, strong correlations can be rendered based on what would otherwise be relatively small sample sizes.

Simulation and mediation both take on unavoidable roles in such research procedures, where neural correlates of one individual's thoughts and memories are inferred from traces of metabolic energy flows, which are, in turn, translations of electrical currents and algorithms processed through digital machines. This method is far from "noise proof," with each brain-image being the result of a highly complex series of *signals* that must be able to be *read* alternately by humans and digital technologies in order for this data to be processed into the pictures included with the published research. As Dumit (2004) explains, "the final conceptual object, the *brain-set*, is analogous to the cognitive neuroscience assumption that the brain itself is analyzable into separate module-like components that are differentially active in a state-like manner" (p. 80). Here, brain images serve as the cultural artifacts that neuroscientists employ to sustain the logic underlying their version of auto-individuation.[4] Going further, he suggests "The PET apparatus builds these neuroscience assumptions into its architecture and thus cam *appear* to confirm them, while necessarily reinforcing them" (p. 81).

Dumit (2004) also underscores how datasets from brain imaging have proven to be significantly more difficult to interpret than expected due to a growing range of unforeseen variables. He points to research suggesting that maps of what should otherwise be similarly appearing activity in the same brain can vary notably depending on, for instance, the time of day the scan was taken. A consequential degree of "noise" has likewise been detected based purely on the handedness of research participants. In other words, whether a participant is right-hand or left-hand dominant can skew how images of brain activity are generated in unpredictable ways. In this sense, the validity of cognitive neuroscientific research is unavoidably constrained by: (1) the limits of their own tools, which require highly rote tasks to avoid adding too much "noise"; (2) the series of methodological decisions made during brain-imaging process, with each one having possible effects on the data; and (3) the fidelity of the extant brain research, where participants have been predominately WEIRD (western, educated, industrialized, rich, and democratic).

This illustrates a certain artificial structure—perhaps, even, an artificial intelligence—underpinning the myth of cerebral-individuation in terms of how it captures its object (i.e., the brain) with very little understanding of the person whose head the object is located. "Artificial," in this sense, can be understood as an extension of Simondon's definition above, where constitutive elements of an ensemble remain dependent on the overarching structure in which they were initially fashioned for human use. Given how many links of technical and interpretive mediation are required to fill in the neurological gaps between environmental stimulus and measured response, it is worth questioning exactly who's imagination brain images represent—the observer or the observed? The availability of computers to model reality in these ways has utterly transformed the ways scientists operate; this, in turn, provides new models of science for scientists to reinterpret themselves. There is a distinctly cybernetic logic involved in how cognitive neuroscience determines neural correlates for behaviors by comparing datasets from an individual PET with an *atlas* based on a "generalized brain," prior to introjecting the significance of such neural correlates into the profiles of altogether different individuals.

Edwin Hutchins (2010) links cybernetics directly to the development computational models of the mind in a slightly different way, explaining that:

> Cyberneticists like Bateson were interested in information, but they emphasized the fact that the information loops that constitute mind extend through the body into the world. This view forced an acknowledgement of the roles of the body and the world in thinking. Meanwhile, advocates of an information processing approach [*ala* Claude Shannon's MTC] saw the digital computer as a model of mind and sought to explain cognition by reduction to internal symbolic events. (p. 707)

By Hutchins' account, symbolic processing models largely came out on top, pushing second-order cybernetic approaches like Bateson's to the margins. Still, the dominant paradigm in cognitive neuroscience today construes "the brain… as a controller of the body [and mind] rather than a computer implemented in meat" (p. 707). While digital computers might provide a useful metaphor for cognitive scientists to think about thinking, a more general emphasis on cybernetic control has thus become an overarching lens for thinking about how the cerebral cortex of the brain (the area most often linked to consciousness and other "higher order" processes) serves as a sort of "manager" of the rest of the brain/body.

Within such myths of cerebral-individuation, neurological impulses underpinning behavior are not only internalized to the individual, as they were with psychoanalysis, but linked to a specific region—the cerebral cortex—of an idealized map of the brain. Such impulses are not considered causes for behavior themselves; they are merely discrete links in chains of continuous reactions of neural firing—a process that is, again, heavily mediated by technology and human interpretation. Here, human agency is coded in terms of a certain degree of cerebral control over performance error; with performance success being defined empirically, in relation to the existing research literature on a particular rote task that happens to be replicable under the limitations of methods in cognitive neuroscience. With the concept of impulse fully digitized in terms of an all-or-nothing principle, and the individual unit of the "neuron" packaged in a cerebral system of control, such methods have nonetheless constructed a custom-made framework for carrying out many useful forms of research on computer-human interface. This involves digitization on various levels, from the binary model of the neuron itself to the unavoidable gaps between datasets that brain-imaging technologies collect.

To be clear, then, this is not to imply that cognitive neuroscience is entirely wrong about the importance of its unit of analysis or that its methods should be discarded altogether in favor of others. To the contrary, there are irreducibly important relationships between brains, human behavior, and social contexts worth exploring. Still, it is important to weigh the growing social value of neurological imaging technologies against the limits inherent to the knowledge they produce, particularly when it comes to how such knowledge is applied to clinical or any other non-academic purpose. PET scans can have direct social consequences outside of laboratory settings, for instance, altering trials and directing clinical decisions related to mental distress. While psychological knowledge has traditionally relied on a human mediator, or observer (i.e., clinician or researcher), to interpret data and apply it in a socially conscious way, one of the stated visions for emerging data-centered mental health is to bypass the universal need for human mediation by using technologies like machine learning software to identify human problems and intervene accordingly (see Luxton, 2015). Here, the computer—programmed as it is by groups of professionals and computer scientists—both collects the data and carries out the intervention, thus fulfilling many of the stated goals of early cybernetic theorists.

Regarding the "the analogy between the cybernetic domain and the cerebral domain," in particular, Catherine Malabou (2012) suggests that it "rests on the idea that thinking amounts to calculating, and calculating to programming" (p. 34). What such a perspective essentially overlooks is the way agency is not localizable anywhere in the brain. The "thinking self," in other words, does not reside in the cerebral cortex or any other area. Agency is distributed throughout not only the entirety of the brain but moreover the body while participating in complex sociolinguistic processes with other agencies throughout the world. And in this way, the network complexity of the brain mirrors that of language and social networks generally. As described by Macy attendee Hans von Foerster (2007), for instance:

> Reflecting on the magic of language is similar to reflecting upon a theory of the brain. As much as one needs a brain to reflect upon a theory of the brain, one needs the magic of language to reflect upon the magic of language. It is the magic of those notions that they need themselves to come into being. They are of second-order. It is also the way language protects itself against explanation by always speaking about itself. (von Foerster, 2007, p. 296)

Unfortunately for cognitive neuroscientists, interactions between agents in complex social situations typically do not conform to the task simplicity required to conduct brain-imaging research. And in the end, to have conversations about such processes requires that some*body* is present to draw boundaries between one system and another; otherwise, there are simply raw, material flows of energy through circuits that do not have a beginning or end (which might be the most objective representation of the brain there is). The yet answered, and perhaps unanswerable, questions regarding myths of cerebral-individuation are thus related to where these distinctions should be made as well as who should determine how such boundaries impact individuals' everyday lives. Or, as Malabou (2012) asks: "What should we do with our brain?"

Notes

1 In his seminars on the *Psychoanalytic Act*, Jacques Lacan (1967) notes "the way in which in the course of [Pavlov's] experiments we never receive from the experimenters the least testimony of what is involved and which, nevertheless, must exist, in the personal relations…between the animal and the experimenter" (p. 26). Lacan goes on to say that, "the link from Signifier to Signifier in so far as we know it to be subjectifying in its nature is introduced by Pavlov in the very setting up of the experiment" (p. 26).

2 This use of the term organism has a significant ideological history well before behaviorism. As Georges Canguilheim (1989) explains:

> The history of the concept of organism in the 18th century can be summed up as the search, by naturalists, physicians and philosophers, for replacement or semantic equivalents for the soul, which could account for the increasingly well-established fact of the functional unity of a system of integrated parts. (p. 551)

3 McCulloch and Pitts were careful to acknowledge "that their definition of a neuron was idealized, and that they made physical assumptions that were 'most convenient for the calculus' (c.f. McCulloch & Pitts 1943, p. 116)" (Abraham,

2002, p. 21). For them, neural circuits were composed of an irreducibly complex combination of digital and analog processes, and it would be inaccurate to characterize brain activity according to either set.
4 George Miller's (2004) critique of Shannon's information theory is relevant here, as well, insofar as "[i]nformation measurement is based on probabilities and increasingly the probabilities seemed more interesting than their logarithmic values, and neither the probabilities nor their logarithms shed much light on the psychological processes that were responsible for them" (p. 141).

4
DEINSTITUTIONALIZATION, BIOPOLITICS, AND NETWORK MAPS OF "MENTAL DISORDER"[1]

Introduction

There is no shortage of critical research linking the history of psychiatry to governmentality and social power (e.g., Fanon, 2008; Foucault, 2008; Whitaker, 2019). Such accounts typically frame psychiatric practices and concepts as technologies used initially by Western governments, but increasingly others as well (see Mills, 2014), to impose order on individuals whose behaviors do not conform to conventional cultural norms. Such histories might point to a range of formally oppressive psychiatric diagnoses, like *drapetomania*, the "runaway slave syndrome," or various iterations of female *hysteria*, as examples of how such psychiatric technologies have been used to support contemporary forms of social oppression. It has also been common for psychiatrists to pathologize non-normative sexual orientations and gender expressions without regard for the desires of the diagnosed persons (Zucker & Spitzer, 2005).

As historian Janet Tighe (1992) noted decades ago, however, "[i]t is no longer novel or provocative to begin an analysis of psychiatric thinking with comments about the 'social construction' of mental illness" (p. 207). Across nearly all fields related to psychopathology, she explains, it has been acknowledged that existing public policy, cultural norms, and even the idiosyncratic cognitive processes of individual scientist practitioners can exert some degree of influence over the "complex and subtle process[es] of negotiation" involved in defining and diagnosing mental disorders (p. 207). The more pressing and, perhaps, more interesting questions here are related to how it is that mental health professionals do, in fact, successfully intervene on biological processes, and who benefits most from how these practices are organized?

This chapter builds on the histories traced so far to illustrate how psychological theories of motivation and behavioral control—the myths of auto-individuation outlined in Chapter 3—have played key roles in the evolution of mental health care in America. Starting similarly with psychoanalysis, the history of psychiatry can be defined by a series of innovations that have allowed causes of observed behaviors to be mapped and intervened upon according to networks of relations that are only partially observable in ways that usually require the aid of technology. The technologies that psychiatric practices have incorporated into their models, however, are even more directly interventive than technologies used throughout the history of psychology. In addition to diagnostic taxonomies, like the DSM and ICD, this includes biomedical technologies ranging from surgeries to psychopharmaceuticals. Together, such technologies contribute to a mechanistic model of mental health, where those working within certain social institutions are granted the authority to code individual behaviors as biological (either neurological or genetic) defects and translate them into a certain degree of social risk.

There are two closely related historical trends that stand out as especially important to the ways mental health and disorder have become re-envisioned through cybernetics and information theories. The first is what has come to be referred to as the deinstitutionalization of psychiatry. Here, services that had been rendered exclusively in psychiatric institutions became decentralized in ways that distributed them across a diverse array of social settings (e.g., schools, workplaces, prisons). With this, ideas about mental health were shaped and continually reshaped to meet the respective social purposes of any organization where they were applied. Principles of behavior modification have served a central role throughout this process, as well, insofar as such social technologies can be tailored to the specific needs of social institutions.

At the same time, the deinstitutionalization of psychiatry would not have been possible had it not corresponded with another trend: the co-emergence of neuroscience and psychopharmacology as new frameworks for making sense of mental health. This initiated a wide-scale paradigm shift in psychiatry from psychoanalysis to new biomedical models. However, causes for psychopathology since then have been notoriously difficult to confirm (see Deacon, 2013). Questions about the legitimacy of diagnostic categories are thus often determined by their clinical utility as opposed to scientific validity or reliability, contributing to another myth of auto-individuation in the form of a biomedical model of mental health.

Not coincidentally, cybernetics and information theories have proven useful here, as well, insofar as they provide a general language for psychologists and health care professionals to more effectively quantify relations across brain activity, behaviors of organisms, and the goals of social institutions. Once a method was available to effectively translate human behaviors into a series of digital computations, it became possible, in turn, for computer scientists and other AI researchers to learn from the human brain to create more complex hardware systems for their own digital purposes. And yet, the explanatory capacity of the *brain as digital computer* metaphor, and its practical applications in altering human behavior, has likely exceeded the scope of even what those like McCulloch and Pitts could have imagined possible. The biomedical model of psychiatry has without question become the dominant approach taken in most mental health contexts around the world. Problems in everyday life have become described increasingly in terms of electrochemical processes within individual brains. Psychopharmaceutical interventions targeting neurotransmitter functions at the synapses of brains have become more popular than ever before.

With growing emphasis in recent decades on notions like empirically supported interventions and evidence-based practices (Bearman et al., 2015), there is in turn a broader effort to create new maps of diagnoses, intervention processes, and treatment outcomes—whether this be through computer images, data graphs, charts, or other statistical representations. The very idea of prioritizing mental health practices based on empirical evidence (i.e., data) implies that care is more likely to be successful if certain sets of prescriptions are followed rather than others. However, this assumes in turn that treatment programs can be standardized across different populations of service-users, regardless of issues related to race, gender, and class, and, as if treatment programs were social technologies that can simply be replicated without regard for culture and context. Both these assumptions have come under increased scrutiny as of late (Mills, 2014; Karter & Kamens, 2019).

The group who tends to be affected most by such trends, moreover, are children, particularly those of color. Mental health outcomes and poverty in childhood are closely linked, and children of color experience poverty at rates 2–3 times higher than white children (Pew Research Center, 2015). Recently, the concept of neuroplasticity has been applied in attempts to analyze these trends, effectively recasting childhood problems stemming from poverty in neurobiological terms (Pitts-Taylor, 2019). Such claims also draw heavily on brains scans as their primary source of data. The assertion is that children in poverty do not simply suffer from additional life challenges that other children, but that such challenges can (sometimes permanently) alter their brains to the extent they lose neural flexibility they would have otherwise had. Given what we know about brain-imaging, however, there it is simply not possible to draw this link conclusively based on such datasets exclusively. This points to a bigger problem, where the mental and emotional states of those who are socially oppressed are coded into medical terms in ways that oversimply complex structural problems, like poverty and racism.

This is just a brief sketch of some of the most important issues at state when thinking about the increasing biomedicalization of mental health. Rather than focusing specifically on how theories about the human mind have changed throughout this process, however, this chapter builds upon earlier ones to explore how diagnostic and interventive technologies used by mental health professionals have evolved alongside certain industries that have staked a claim in their market. This sets a foundation for next chapter, which explores how ideas in psychology applied to mental health have become pre-packaged in forms that can be distributed across a growing variety of social contexts all over the world; in other words, I illustrate how technologies related to "mental health" have become further decentralized, largely through information technologies.

From deinstitutionalization to the decentralization of mental health

At the beginning of the 1950s, the landscape of mental health care in America looked considerably different than it does today. Psychiatrists worked primarily in hospitals and other state-run institutions. No prescription drugs had been approved by the FDA to combat symptoms of psychological distress. The most common "treatments" were lobotomies, insulin shots, and electro-convulsive therapies. While some psychiatrists were optimistic that such treatments would provide a solid biological basis for their field, they all functioned to produce the same basic effect—create more passive patients who were considered less likely to pose threats to themselves or others. There was little impression on the part of anyone working in such intuitions that serious mental health problems could be cured, and most who came under institutionalized care remained so throughout the duration of their lives.

By the end of the 1950s, however, mental health care in America had gone through a series of radical structural changes. In 1952, the first edition of the DSM was published, providing a general manual to guide clinical decision making in psychiatry. It was based largely on a biopsychological approach developed Adolf Meyer, a psychoanalytically orientated clinician (Shorter, 2015). Another major turning point occurred in May 1954, when the drug chlorpromazine was introduced into the U.S. market under the name Thorazine (Whitaker, 2019). For the first time ever, a pharmacological agent was available to psychiatrists to alter the behaviors of their patients. Many current psychiatrists consider this latter development nothing short of a revolution in the field of psychiatry. Shorter (1998), for instance, compares it to the "introduction of penicillin in general medicine" (p. 255), with Rollin (1990) praising how it "tore through the civilized world like a whirlwind and engulfed the whole treatment spectrum of psychiatric disorders" (p. 113). From 1953 to 1961, federal spending on mental health care increased from $10.9 million to $100.9 million, fueled largely by hopeful narratives about the potential of newly created "anti-psychotic" drugs (Whitaker, 2019). A new "mental health" market was thus created in which private industries could invest for their own respective reasons.

At the same time, scrutiny began to mount regarding the inhumane conditions inside most psychiatric hospitals. Although institutionalized psychiatry always has always had its detractors (see, for example, Bly, 2012), the mid-20th century witnessed various anti-psychiatry activists—ranging from R.D. Laing, Ervin Goffman, and Thomas Szasz—speaking out forcefully in demand of radical alternatives. By the early 1960s, movements to deinstitutionalize mental health care were in full force. In 1963, President Kennedy's *Community Mental Health Centers Construction Act* redirected funds to create more community mental health options, despite tying such funds to increased research on psychopharmaceuticals due to the exciting potential he saw in them. The term "deinstitutionalization" thus came to represent a broad, international coalition across diverse service users, providers, politicians, and private industries. Despite each interest group having notably different goals and purposes, they were all united by an overarching aim to make mental health care more uniquely tailored to each local context.

The concerted efforts to deinstitutionalize psychiatry also overlapped historically and conceptually with a wide-scale paradigm shift in American psychiatry away from psychoanalysis. In the first half of the 20th century, as analysts emigrated from Europe during the two world wars, and Freud's nephew popularized his ideas as marketing tools (Justman, 1994), psychoanalysis gradually became the dominant framework in America for thinking about people in general. As psychopharmaceutical agents became more popular, however, psychoanalysis began falling out of favor in psychiatry and a neo-Kraepelinian (biomedical) model emerged to take its place (Shorter, 2015). Unsurprisingly, such changes were pushed by health insurers and pharmaceutical companies as much as the American Psychiatric Association or any other governing body (Mayes & Horwitz, 2005; Pilecki et al., 2011). In 1980, the publication of the third edition of the DSM punctuated this transition by providing a more complex, descriptive taxonomy of mental disorders. Here, disorders were transformed "from broad, etiologically defined entities that were continuous with normality" to "symptom-based, categorical diseases" (Mayes & Horwitz, 2005, p. 249).

The paradigm-shift away from psychoanalytic explanations for mental suffering likewise drew a new line in the sand between research and practice. Despite the DSM-III dropping all reference to etiology, prominent psychiatrists proclaimed its publication represented "a reaffirmation on the part of American psychiatry to its medical identity and its commitment to scientific medicine" (Klerman et al., 1984, p. 539). Such an explicit alignment with other medical professions reinforced existing beliefs that the new research-practice divide would be bridged naturally by advances in neuroscience and research on psychopharmaceutical drugs. Research based on the McCulloch and Pitts (1943) model of neural activity, introduced last chapter, implicitly undergird many of such assumptions. With the notion of brain activity as series of events across synapses, psychiatrists have been able to re-envision the target of their interventions in terms of communication *via* neurotransmitters between neurons. Advancements in brain technology, moreover, have led to all sorts of maps of such neural activity, which have come to be used liberally, in turn, to make sense of changes in human behavior. Consequently, communication between service providers and users now serves as but one of several mediators between diagnosis and treatment—a stark contrast from psychoanalysis and other forms of talk therapy, where interaction with clients is a direct form of intervention.

Throughout the course of these changes, the DSM has come to serve a much wider range of social purposes, allowing organizations that provide services to more efficiently code individual behaviors, grouping them by diagnosis, and distribute resources accordingly. It is thus impossible to understand the deinstitutionalization of mental health services and the evolution of the DSM apart from each other. The DSM is now the primary administrative tool used to coordinate action and facilitate communication across the variety of contexts in which mental health services are provided (see Tsou, 2015). It has come to inform the practices of an exceedingly larger range of professionals—including social workers, professional counselors, clinical psychologists, special educators, and other care administrators—with each group using the DSM for notably different social purposes. This is, importantly, a form of decentralization of mental health services, given how care practices are now distributed and embedded in ways that would not be possible without the changes occurring across the last three editions of DSM.

Despite psychiatric hospitals and asylums closing across the country, and a broad array of new psychotropic drugs being developed, public funds that Kennedy initially earmarked for community mental health centers in America were never delivered. By 1977, there were just around 650 of such centers open across the country—not even half of what was called for by Kennedy's bill. There was renewed hope for wider funding with President Carter's *Mental Health Systems Act*, signed into law in 1980. Unsurprisingly, Carter's bill was quickly repealed by President Reagan just one year later. With public funds for community mental health redirected, private industries positioned themselves in a more determinative role regarding how mental health care would be provided. Today, community mental health services remain underfunded, with a broad reliance on psychopharmaceutical drugs, on the one hand, and the prison industrial complex, on the other, filling this obvious void in care (Whitaker, 2019).

Large amounts of funding continue to be poured into research on the brain each year, and yet specific biological mechanisms underlying most diagnoses in the DSM have yet to be found (Deacon, 2013). To be clear, this does not mean that no *correlations* between mental suffering and biology or genetics have been established (see Panksepp, 2004). It is simply that the categories in the DSM do not appear group individuals reliably enough for researchers to adequately study them as empirical objects (Tabb, 2015). In the rare cases that a single biological cause has been found for any category in the DSM, moreover—as with Rhett's syndrome following the publication DSM-IV—it will likely be removed entirely from the subsequent version on the basis it is no longer considered a "mental disorder."

This points to something important about the broader structural organization of the DSM and the processes through which diagnostic criteria are perpetually reconfigured. According to the APA (2013), the goal is for such categories to facilitate with procedures of *differential diagnosis*. This means that the criteria for any one diagnosis in the DSM is contingent on its ability to be differentiated from other diagnoses. In this way, systems of classification or representation can be constructed, and reconstructed, in ways that provide common denominators for professionals and researchers across diverse social fields. As Volkmar and Rechow (2013) explain, more stringent differential criteria are almost always helpful from a clinical perspective because it helps professionals "communicate more effectively about clinical problems (rapidly conveying a general sense of the kinds of difficulties exhibited) and conduct better research" (para. 1). Even if clinicians are well aware that diagnoses are never going to serve as perfect representations of their clients and/or patients, the categorical structures (i.e., taxonomies) diagnoses form with each other nonetheless facilitate communication between professionals and researchers who might share common, or at least overlapping, goals.

This has spurred researchers, like Kathryn Tabb (2015), to propose that such an epistemic gap between research (operationalizability) and practice (interpretive flexibility) might not be inherently problematic if clinical researchers are willing to drop their commitments to *diagnostic discrimination*. This can be understood as "the assumption that our diagnostic tests group patients together in ways that allow for relevant facts about mental disorder to be discovered" (pp. 1049). Such commitments tend to presuppose that diagnostic categories are natural kinds (see Hacking, 2000), obscuring how they function as social heuristics. Through commitments to notions like interrater reliability, diagnostic categories are all too often judged against empirical standards that belie their social utility as flexible clinical tools. Tabb also underscores that it is becoming increasingly common, and in fact useful, to approach clinical research with new models that map criteria beyond what the DSM can reasonably be expected to address. For her, this provides important avenues for scientists and philosophers to "investigate the ways in which psychiatry stabilizes its diverse objects of research across disciplinary boundaries in the absence of the DSM's authoritative voice" (p. 1058).

The National Institute of Mental Health, under the guidance of Thomas Insel, has recently begun developing just such a classification system under the title of Research Domain Criteria (RDoC). The idea is to use exclusively dimensional criteria to chart general domains of human functioning (i.e., positive valence systems, negative valence systems, cognitive systems, social systems, and arousal/regulatory systems). All such domains are integrated into a common matrix that, similar to the first two editions of the DSM, positions mental disorders on scales that are continuous with normality. Indeed, the NIMH makes it clear that the

> RDoC framework is explicitly agnostic with respect to current definitions of disorders ... studying the individual mechanisms may lead to better understanding of current disorders, or perhaps new and

novel definitions of disorders, but in either case improved information about treatment choices. (para. 6)

And yet, it remains unclear how the domains of research connected to RDoC will aid with clinical processes, given how it is so important for them to be tailored to unique situations. Domain criteria are defined through large-scale data collection and interpretation efforts, which constitute a very different form of social practice than mental health care. Unless diagnoses based on domain criteria are continually updated as new data are gathered, with all mental health professionals granted access to, trained to interpret, and agreeing to use such information uniformly, the epistemic gap between research (operationalization) and practice (interpretive flexibility) is likely be reproduced in ever-more complex forms. With the goal being to ground such criteria in general maps of neural circuitry (Cuthbert & Insel, 2013), the ontological gaps overviewed throughout this book (e.g., between observer and observed) are yet unacknowledged issues for RDoC. And as Cosgrove and Karter (2018) remind us, such gaps are not value-neutral—ignorance about what mental disorders are has long been capitalized on by organizations in positions to profit from the commodification and expansion of mental health care.

In general, the ongoing process of deinstitutionalization of mental health care involves a broad range of moving parts, with professionals and service users often disagreeing on the best route to take moving forward (Johnstone & Boyle et al., 2018). This is another reason it could be helpful to reinterpret the history of psychiatry through the lens of systems theories in the vein of cybernetics. As Enric Novella (2010) explains:

> the wider deployment of the modern social order as a functionally differentiated system may be considered to be a consistent driving force for [deinstitutionalization]; it has made asylum psychiatry overly incompatible with prevailing social values (particularly with the normative and regulative principle of inclusion of all individuals in the different functional spheres of society and with the common patterns of participation in modern function systems) and has, in turn, required the availability of psychiatric care for a growing number of individuals. (p. 411)

Insofar as mental health services today must be rendered across widely different types of social settings, a standardized vocabulary with flexible rules for inclusion seems necessary given the practical realities of deinstitutionalized care. With narratives about causes for psychopathology becoming ever-more obscure, it has been easier for private companies to step in and capitalize on the mounting fear and uncertainty. As outlined in more detail below, this is likewise how Western values related to mental health have been packaged with progressive values to be shipped as myths of auto-individuation across a growing number of cultures and social institutions around the world. This is, again, how mental health is becoming increasingly decentralized.

Biomedical neoliberalism and the ongoing cooption of deinstitutionalized care

Despite all the confusion surrounding causes for psychopathology outlined above, the most common approach in mental health care continues to be a biomedical one that assumes: (a) there are biological causes for the diagnoses codified in the DSM and (b) medical interventions are typically the best options available. The latter of these two beliefs is common even among those who are critical of the DSM, with Thomas Insel, for instance, lamenting "the absence of biomarkers, the lack of valid diagnostic categories, and our limited understanding of the biology of these illnesses [which makes] targeted medication development especially difficult for mental disorders" (2011, para. 8). And yet, he claims elsewhere that "[m]any illnesses previously defined as "mental" are now recognized to have a biological cause" (2007, p. 757). Understood together, such statements appear to be an attempt to incentivize future brain research so that, as Insel suggests elsewhere, "clinical neuroscience can eventually replace the practice of psychiatry, not with less of a commitment to clinical excellence but with a great commitment to developing a new scientific basis for clinical care" (2012, para. 7). This is also why he considers projects like RDoC so important.

Returning to the discussion about cognitive neuroscience in Chapter 3, however, there are many reasons for reservation regarding statements like Insel's above. For clinical neuroscience to replace psychiatry, for instance, the bare minimum criteria should be an accurate method to accurately correlate various regions of the brain and their neurotransmitter activity with human behaviors, ideally even thoughts and emotions. And yet, as Dumit (2004) explains:

> [f]unctional brain regions do not exist in the brain where neurons are in constant cross-talk with each other using a variety of electrical, chemical, and physiological means at spatial scales of nanometers

and time scales of nanoseconds. Instead, the PET apparatus produces the functional brain region as a discrete, measurable, locatable, and ideally namable time-space voxel of the brain that can be correlated with the person's state or trait. (p. 79)

In other words, clinical neuroscientists champion their work because the human brain is one of the most complex objects on Earth; yet, precisely because it is so complex, it is impossible to represent it accurately in digital terms. Going further, Dumit lists over 30 different possible confounding variable identified across a short list of articles that attempt to relate PET results to "mental illness," ranging from "time of day" and "failure to control for gender and age differences" to "state vs. trait descriptions," "assumption that subjects with illness exhibit a pattern of regular metabolism that can distinguish them from normal subject," and "cycling patterns of psychosis/relative normality may not be captured or reproducible with 30-minute glimpses of metabolism" (p. 102). Any one of these issues, if not somehow *controlled* for quite enough, could render an entire dataset meaningless.

Another reason that identifying causes for mental disorders has proven so difficult is that general assumptions about psychopathology have been shaped heavily by the treatments used most often (see Thomas et al., 2019). Since the 1950s, hundreds of different psychiatric medications have been produced in the forms of antipsychotics, antidepressants, anxiolytics, mood stabilizers, and stimulants. And yet, there has been a notable dearth of significant research results to date attributing diagnoses, as they are codified in the DSM, to obvious biological or genetic causal mechanisms (see Deacon, 2013). What this essentially means is that terms like "antipsychotic" and "antidepressant" are misnomers. No single prescription can treat every symptom of any single disorder; it can simply produce noticeable effects in the way some symptoms are experienced. Although, even here, recent research suggests only marginal benefits for most who actually respond favorably to anti-depressants (Hengartner et al., 2019), with growing rates of polypharmacy in recent decades linked to both higher mortality rates and lower quality of life (Kukreja et al., 2013).

This has led to a curious situation where "nearly every major pharmaceutical company has either reduced greatly or abandoned research and development of mechanistically novel psychiatric drugs" (Fibiger, 2012, p. 649); though they are still sustaining high profits largely by marketing new uses for old drugs (Whitaker & Cosgrove, 2015). Steady prescription rates seem to suggest that drugs are working to do something, perhaps just not what people generally assume they do. This likewise seems to be the case for diagnostic categories in the DSM. Here, diagnostic categories, myths of auto-individuation, and psychopharmaceuticals have all proven useful social technologies precisely because they can be applied to such a broad range of different problems. And yet, problems are not value neutral, and as such, it is important to reflect critically on how, and by whom, such problems are defined. Almost all the early psychopharmaceutical drugs, for instance, were neuroleptics, meaning they operated to block neurotransmitter activity in ways that often corresponded with decreased (or flat) affect and general apathy (Whitaker, 2019). Many of the drugs currently prescribed for psychosis work in similar ways. Then there are selective serotonin reuptake inhibitors (SSRIs), for instance, which work by blocking the reuptake the neurotransmitter, serotonin, so that it stays in the synapse (exerting an effect) longer, and finally amphetamines, which increase dopamine and norepinephrine. The primary mechanisms thus modulate specific chemicals, and hence general affect, through inhibition or amplification (a binary − or +).

A popular assumption underpinning the broad use of such drugs is that neurotransmitter activity underpins the most important human functions. In this sense, the logic of biomedical models construct their notion of "the individual" *as* neural activity—at least as far as controlling for external "noise" is concerned. By isolating the functions of neurotransmitters and finding the right combination of inhibitors and catalysts to modulate them, the hope is that various combinations of psychotropic drugs should one day provide the perfect mechanisms of control over each individual person's unwanted thoughts, emotions, and/or behaviors. This line of reasoning would make sense if there were a clear 1:1 correspondence between brain states and mental states. As outlined so far, however, this is clearly not the case. While the activity of respective neurotransmitters can be correlated loosely with certain emotions, behaviors, or experiences, the precise nature of these relationships can vary quite a lot from person to person. This is another area where the ontological gap between first-person and third-person perspectives is central to how we think about mental distress. This is also why it is so important to render the logic underlying biomedical treatments explicit. Here, questions about ontology, epistemology, and economics unavoidably intertwined through the ways mental disorders are classified, diagnosed, and treated, as "what you think a mental disorder is reflexively affects how you think it can come to be known, understood, or measured" (Karter & Kamens, 2019, p. 27).

Mounting research confirms that mental suffering is clearly linked to a wide range of potential causes, which are not always explained best by biology or neuroscience (Johnstone & Boyle et al., 2018). With such a wide range of factors obviously involved in any instance of mental suffering, a central question to pose to clinical researchers today is why proceed *as if* biological causes are the most viable target of research and intervention? Gomory et al. (2011) explore this question, as well, noting how:

> ...problems previously attributed to environmental, social, and personal factors—such as poverty, disintegration of family and community, grueling work, and abusive or neglectful childhood—have been increasingly attributed to brain dysfunctions stemming from as-of-yet-unconfirmed genetic and chemical defects. (p. 1)

Even in circumstances where adequate empirical evidence is lacking, they suggest, there is a notable tendency to reduce distinct and complex forms of psychosocial suffering to a circumscribed set of assumed biological causes. What is perhaps most problematic here, however, is that such causes are popularly proposed throughout biomedical studies as explanations—rather than mere descriptions—for atypical behaviors or neurological types. Anytime complex psychosocial experiences are reduced to biological explanations, otherwise useful social interventions in the form of policy change or direct political are often marginalized in favor of medical treatment (Thomas et al., 2019). This is especially true when Western models of mental health are transported to different areas of the world (Kirmayer & Pedersen, 2014).

In these ways, stakes in the future of mental health care have become linked to what are, increasingly, transnational biomedical markets (see Cosgrove & Karter, 2018). Some mental health professionals have gone as far as to describe this evolving network of biomedical research and practice in terms of a biomedical industrial complex, since mental health services have effectively been monopolized by biomedical industries cutting across a variety of social contexts (see, for instance, Lacasse, 2014). In coding a growing range of possible causes for mental disorder intro neurobiological and genetic terms, narratives around responsibility and agency regarding treatment have been reconfigured to reflect broader neoliberal values (Thomas et al., 2019). Here, the survival of certain organizations often comes to assume priority over the quality of care, since without the organization receiving funding (so the argument goes) there can be no care. It is thus not only the concepts and practices in psy-disciplines that have been hollowed out and replaced with codes for generating capital, but also the operations of many broader institutions in which they are applied.

On top of all this, studies that challenge the exclusivity of a biomedical paradigm of mental health tend to be marginalized in the curriculum of many of degree programs for social workers (Lacasse & Gomory, 2003)— the profession of service providers who use the DSM most often in practice (Gomory et al., 2011). In a broader sense, it seems, many of the social institutions providing health care and other public services in earlier generations are simply no longer operating in the same ways they used to. Gilles Deleuze (1992) describes a similar notion in terms of a:

> …generalized crisis in relation to all the environments of enclosure— prison, hospital, factory, school, family. The family is an "interior" in crisis like all other interiors—scholarly, professional, etc. The administrations in charge never cease announcing supposedly necessary reforms: to reform schools, to reform industries, hospitals, the armed forces, prisons. But everyone knows these institutions are finished, whatever the length of their expiration periods. It's only a matter of administering their last rites and of keeping people employed until the installation of new forces knocking at the door. (p. 3–4)

With public trust in such bedrock institutions steadily eroding, any resources they still have to offer have gradually been repurposed for overarching demands to observe and intervene on individual behaviors. For professionals working across institutions like schools, hospitals, prisons, and government agencies, there is no longer the sense of job security there once was. There is, to the contrary, simply ongoing conversations about budget cuts or potential downsizing in a certain department. The risks are many and they are always just around the corner.

One area where such hollowing out has become especially obvious is in the way insurance reimbursement for most mental health services has become dependent on the DSM. The current protocol for insurance companies in America is to require a set of billing codes from those listed alongside each diagnosis in the DSM on any paperwork clinicians file to for services to be covered. For anyone to use their insurance plan to receive mental health services, in other words, they must be given at least one diagnosis in the DSM. This can unquestionably put clinicians in ethically compromising positions (see Barbash, 2017). If a client of theirs seems to benefit from therapy, for instance, but it might not rise to the level of "medical necessity," as determined by insurance companies themselves, clinicians could legally be committing fraud by giving them a diagnosis.

Some clinicians have thus refused to accept insurance altogether because of what they view as unethical data confidentiality practices of insurance companies. According to Barbash (2017), for instance,

> The insurer can also audit your records at any time they wish, which means they have full access to any details your therapist has, including information the therapist intentionally did not include in the claim submitted to the insurance company. Any and all information, including progress notes, which can include details about what occurred during the therapy session, is technically open to the claim's specialist. (para. 16)

While it is illegal to share personal health information directly—including information about mental health—it can become coded in ways that still convey important details that could affect a person's life later. For instance, if an individual gets a diagnosis at age 26, it is possible that, based on what information was shared with other insurance companies, or if the same company keeps said data on file, it could bar that person from getting life insurance or some other form of coverage later in life. In these ways, and more, insurance companies have managed to secure increasing amounts of control over how mental health practices are rendered, with clinicians having few options of recourse other than refusing to work with a certain insurance company moving forward. And yet, if every clinician did this then therapy (at what can sometimes be as high as 200 dollars a session) would essentially be reserved for the upper-class.

Given that, on the one hand, diagnoses codified in the DSM are considered to have such low inter-rater reliability (Lacasse, 2014) and, on the other hand, biomarkers for most of them have been hard to come by (Deacon, 2013), it is curious why multi-billion dollar industries would rely on them to determine which services a clinician can bill for and for how long they can do so. And yet, this relationship makes much more sense in the context of research by Cosgrove and Krimsky (2012) suggesting that 69% of members on the DSM-5 task force reported having financial ties to the pharmaceutical industry. According to these authors, moreover, this represents "a relative increase of 21% over the proportion of *DSM*-IV task force members with such ties" (para. 4). In general, these overlaps clearly expose concerted efforts across to analyze data on individual's mental health as financial information to avoid risky business decisions moving forward, and this occurs largely beyond the control of those individuals from whom such data is collected.

The risk-orientated narratives around which mental health practices have been organized represent some of the most obvious ways in which cybernetic principles have exerted transformed contemporary social institutions. But of course, risk-averse practices have come to be at the basis of most organizations today. Sociologist Anthony Giddens illustrates such trends by starting many of his public talks, for instance, with the following thought experiment:

> What do the following have in common? Mad cow disease; the troubles as Lloyds Insurance; the Nick Leeson affair [at Bearings Bank]; genetically modified crops; global warming; the notion that red wine is good for you; anxieties about declining sperm counts. (c.f. Garland, 2003, p. 48)?

His answer: each of these issues taps into our collective drives, as members of a given society, to foresee and curtail future risk. Giddens (1999) and Ulrich Beck, moreover, (1992) link growing preoccupation with risk to the inherent unpredictability of current world affairs, which they describe as producing, for the very first time, what are essentially "global risks." This mentality is expressed in contemporary global mental health movements, for instance, with Cosgrove and Karter (2018) asking "who 50 years ago could have predicted that depressed people would become a global category?" (p. 672).

While there have always been physical dangers and external hazards present in human environments—likely in greater numbers than today—Giddens (1999) underscores how unrealistically high demands to predict future outcomes, alongside so many burgeoning manufactured, yet still clearly existential hazards (e.g., climate change, nuclear war, etc.), create a new order of anxiety for most individuals across contemporary capitalist societies. Given how such social risks evolve with each new technological innovation, they are impossible to forecast with any degree of certainty. And yet, living in a risk society, as it were, means that we are each required to learn even what "[w]e don't, and we can't, know – yet all of us, as consumers, have to respond in some way or another to this unstable and complex framework of scientific claims and counterclaims" (Giddens, 1999, p. 2). Navigating this landscape successfully thus requires the ongoing maintenance of a certain risk-orientated attitude, whereby any object and/or person one encounters is evaluated largely as a function of any observable risks a relationship with them could potentially entail.

It may well prove useful, then, for contemporary clinicians and psychotherapists to consider the structural limitations of how, as Luhmann (2005) outlines, professionals throughout diverse fields of socioeconomic production are compelled for a variety of reasons to build upon systems of knowledge pertaining to their respective scope of risk; all the while they are, concomitantly, expected to translate the benefits of such expansions into vernaculars and frameworks accessible by other imagined groups. The intensity of demands to extend scopes of institutionally specific risk-assessment is often at its peak at junctures where prior attempts to self-monitor and decrease errors in the technology have failed. This has been argued to be the case with many diagnoses codified in the DSM-5 (see Lacasse, 2014), for instance, and yet the social values underpinning its corresponding boundary infrastructure—in this case, the biomedical industrial complex—remain coded in deficit-based, biomedical terms across clinical practices, scientific studies, and public discourses alike (Pickersgill, 2013). There is thus an underlying logic of paranoia associated with many of such discourses, which only contributes to concerns about various mental health "epidemics" (Wazana et al., 2007).

To quote Cosgrove and Karter (2018), one again, this merely reinforces

> the assumption that individuals' emotional states can be reduced to a universal category and should be monitored because of the social and economic burden of depression, and that market-based surveillance is the most efficient and accurate way to do the monitoring. (p. 676)

As an example of this, they point to how

> Otsuka Pharmaceutical and Proteus Digital Health partnered in 2012 to develop a version of the antipsychotic Abilify that contains a digital sensor that can send real time information about medication compliance, as well as bodily activity patterns, to a medication provider. (p. 676)

The very existence of such digital pills reinforces the lack of trust and autonomy underlying health care relationships more generally. And of all the available pills to roll out such a sensor attached to, it is worth questioning why industry leaders attached it to one that is used primarily to treat psychosis, given how paranoia about being observed by authority is already such a common experience for individuals reporting psychotic symptoms (Rosenbaum, 2017)?

Gray et al. (2013) describe how the diagnosis of autism-spectrum disorders (ASD), for instance, functions to trace trajectories of risk in a double sense: both with "those seen to pose a risk and those considered to be at risk" (p. 1). However, these two domains of risk are often blurred by the general uncertainty regarding autism's status of a neurologically and/or genetically based disorder (Ortega, 2009). ASD represents a notably wide variety of behaviors and modes of expression. As the now popular slogan goes: "If you know about one autistic person, you know about *one* autistic person" (Hacking, 2009, p. 46; original emphasis). And yet, many of the most popular behavioral interventions for ASD can prove especially intensive for both the individuals diagnosed and their family members, even in comparison to treatments for other diagnoses (MacDonald et al., 2014).

Conclusions regarding the success of an intervention are often based on criteria that are often relative to social norms of interaction, such as "measures of eye contact, social engagement, and verbal reciprocity" (Rollins et al., 2015, p. 219). However, popular treatment approaches, predominantly ABA, seem to place the brunt of the burden of any risks allegedly posed by autism on the diagnosed individual, focusing on goals like "shaping skills using rewards (based on what each individual child will 'work' to earn)" (Baron-Cohen, 2008, p. 110). Here, identified "problem" behaviors such as those typically described as "self-stimulatory" (i.e. "stimming"), which have been shown to have idiosyncratic adaptive purposes for those on the spectrum (Connolly, 2008), are encoded into clinical terms with the long-term goal being to replace them with more socially appropriate behaviors. This has led one autistic scholar to ask. Often, this is determined from entirely from the perspective of non-autistic people. This has led autistic scholar Damian Milton (2014) to question, for instance, just "what exactly are autism interventions intervening with?" (p. 6). Factors like poverty, or other environmental stressors are thus often marginalized not because they are unimportant to how ASD is experienced and expressed, but because they cannot be as effectively intervened upon as other levels like brain chemistry and individual behavior.

It is thus not surprising that rates of diagnosis for what the DSM refer to as *neurodevelopmental disorders* have become, by far, the most common type of diagnosis in childhood, especially for those in the criminal justice system (Chitsabesan & Hughes, 2016). Clinically speaking, autism-spectrum disorders ASD tend to be diagnosed based on problems relating to others, either cognitively (i.e., deficits in theory of mind), affectively (i.e., deficits in empathy or sympathy), or both. Attention-deficit hyperactive disorder (ADHD), on the other hand, is generally diagnosed based on a general inability to pay attention in socially appropriate was. Each of these set of determinations, however, is highly context dependent—making any clinical decision-making process dependent on multiple streams of information (e.g., parents, teachers, assessments, etc.)

With such concepts coming to have a greater role in making sense of everyday thoughts and emotions outside of clinical contexts, myths of auto-individuation, in this vein, have taken on a capacity to circulate well beyond the professional contexts in which they were created. It is, for instance, common to see websites circulating a page about "how to know if your child is at-risk for autism" or "tips to know if your child has ADHD." As Meg Evans (2020) describes her own experience with this, as such:

> By late 2003, the picture had grown clear enough that my internal alarm bells were sounding. Those sensational articles hadn't gone away, but instead were showing up more often. Their scope was not limited to children but also encompassed autistic adults, who were commonly described as freakish, incapable, barely human, and unsupportable burdens on society. Internet searches only turned up more of the same, and I began to realize that I was looking at a dangerous mass hysteria.

And yet, despite the way such deficit-based characterizations are premised upon a basic failure to achieve some ideal notion of a normative social relationship, most clinical approaches identify the source of such problems in the brain, while intervening on the brain and behavior together to ameliorate social risks beyond such individuals themselves.

Majia Holmer Nadesan (2013) outlines a similar series of concerns in overviewing a range of contemporary studies and treatments related to autism. Ultimately, she suggests, approaches that are potentially the most profitable, or at least most cost-effective, tend to be funded at higher rates, even in cases where evidence in support of their general clinical efficacy is lacking. In this sense, "disorders such as autism can become business opportunities for bioengineering and pharmaceutical companies" (p. 123). While she is careful to concede that "[n]ot all genetic research is driven by the profit motive" and "not all biological research is genetic," she nonetheless cautions against "the seductive combination of genes and dollars [which] has the potential to crowd out other research trajectories and autism-funding priorities" (p. 123). This is particularly true for those "that might curtail [biomedical] industry profits by foregrounding environmental explanations for autism and other syndromes and diseases" (p. 123).

In other words, insofar as social values across competing markets and diverse institutional settings have become reorganized through a common set of cybernetic principles, any observed behaviors not easily translated into a biomedical vernacular is more likely to be labeled as a disorder and coded in terms of the risks it could pose.

The common conflation of descriptions of biological conditions with explanations for certain experiences, as outlined above, is especially relevant here. An excellent example of this can be found in the description of ADHD given by Insel (2011), below:

> …studies of brain development demonstrate delays in cortical maturation in children with attention deficit hyperactivity disorder. How curious that this disorder, which is defined by cognitive (attention) and behavioral (hyperactivity) symptoms, increasingly appears to be a disorder of cortical development. Viewing ADHD as a brain disorder raises new, important questions: What causes delayed maturation? What treatments might accelerate cortical development? (para. 3)

This is analogous to the move made by behaviorists when they grant agency only to what can be most practically observed and controlled. This provides a clear illustration of the high degree of subjectivity involved in operationalizing variables for any given study. And yet, subjectivity does not imply arbitrariness. Cosgrove and Karter (2018) connect this to

> the assumption that individuals' emotional states can be reduced to a universal category and should be monitored because of the social and economic burden of depression, and that market-based surveillance is the most efficient and accurate way to do the monitoring. (p. 676)

Here, social governance is regulated in the form of first-order cybernetic loops between individual behaviors and the goals of social institutions, but it likewise becomes internalized as a second-order, paranoid frame of reference that each person reinforces themselves by monitoring their own experiences.

Along with others (see, for instance, Teo, 2018), Cosgrove and Karter (2018) situate such trends within broader critiques of neoliberalism—a form of governance that Sugarman (2015) describes as "flexible-capitalism," whereby the:

> key features are a radically free market in which competition is maximized, free trade achieved through economic deregulation,

privatization of public assets, vastly diminished state responsibility over areas of social welfare, the corporatization of human services, and monetary and social policies congenial to corporations and disregardful of the consequences. (p. 104)

Nik-Khah (2017) takes this position, as well, adding that "a peculiar epistemology resides at the heart of the neoliberal worldview. The individual human can never match the epistemic power of markets; therefore, goes the argument, markets should assume primary responsibility for generating knowledge" (p. 3). Insofar as our thoughts, desires, and emotions are observed and intervened upon today more than ever before, effective control over oneself becomes a defining criterion for what it means to be "an individual." A failure to apply such principles of cybernetic rationality successfully to the marketing of oneself, for instance, is not merely a detriment to one's economic prospects (Osbeck, 2004); it can be pathologized on one of many widening spectrums of mental disorder (McGuire, 2017). Osbeck (2004) explains furthermore how forming potentially successful socioeconomic relations with others is often framed in termed of capacities to express a "pleasing personality," which itself "becomes a commodity" (p. 62). She also adds that "[w]e might say that empathy is harnessed in the service of selling the self. Influencing or working with others requires extensive skill in detecting mental states, as does manipulation" (p. 62). Even broader concerns for social issues like the "global burden of depression" (Cosgrove & Karter, 2018, p. 621) have become coopted through neoliberal principles. This essentially represents a wide-scale repurposing of the myth of neural-individuation outlined above, where maps of the brain are decoded in terms of an imaginary individual person who possesses the "normal" model of the brain. But just who has this normal brain and what are the criteria that determine this?

Such questions even become all the more important since the completion of the human genome project. While it did not "decipher the code of human life," as was the promise, it did create a much more complex vision of genetics that has fueled research across different scientific domains, including psychology. Even more relevant to the concerns of this book, however, "the rhetoric of coding and mapping life captured the imagination of national governments and media outlets, resulting in a public visibility rarely enjoyed by scientific initiatives" (Leonelli, 2016, p. 17). Under a largely biomedical frame, the National Institute of Mental Health (NIMH), for instance, has organized one of the world's largest databases for autism related research (the NDAR). As stated on the database summary page, this publicly funded program "aims to accelerate progress in autism spectrum disorder (ASD) research through data sharing, data harmonization, and the reporting of research results" (para. 1). As of August 16, 2016, data pertaining to 127,013 studies and 85,079 individuals overall had been included in the repository. The full array of this research is coded in terms of: (a) gender and phenotypic expression of the subjects and (b) each study's methodological procedure—usually neuroimaging, genomic sequencing, or a combination thereof. The parameters of the database are strictly regulated in the form of a "biomedical informatics system and central repository … [to] provide a common platform for data collection, retrieval and archiving, while allowing for flexibility in data entry and analysis" (U.S. Department of Health and Human Services, 2011, para. 3). The type of studies most often accepted are those with "curated and coded phenotype, exposure, genotype, and pedigree data" (para. 6).

While the stated intention with the NDAR is to better serve those identified with ASD, it is noteworthy that the database is made fully available for public and/or corporate use given any other set of organizational agendas. Additionally, while the database "infrastructure was established initially to support NDAR," it "has grown into an informatics platform that facilitates data sharing across all of mental health and other research communities" (National Institute of Mental Health, para. 7). Such big data networks are often championed as necessary for those in authority to assess potential risks and remain secure in a fast-paced world such as ours. And yet, as the compilation of data grows to proportions that no individual, or even group, could realistically analyze in a single lifetime, what use can it serve other than aggregating the most general trends possible across only the most abstract categories (e.g., gender, age, diagnosis)?

Throughout the history of psychology, there has been no shortage of "black box" models of research where certain areas of human life have been ignored on the basis of historically situated social values, culturally relative assumptions, and/or technological constraints. B.F. Skinner, for instance, described all behavior uniformly across species purely in terms of what could be observed and intervened upon in scientific labs. Not only was information regarding processes internal to the organism excluded, but so was information external to experimental contexts. Along the same lines of such epistemic values, it is common for mental health organizations today to gather information on clients in ways that, while perhaps making it easier to bill insurance and communicate about services, have generally proven unreliable representations of experiences of those diagnosed (see Johnstone & Boyle et al., 2018). In either case, complex sociocultural activities become over-coded in operationalizable terms, often with minimal regard for the range of purposes they might serve within other networks of value or cultural narratives. And in these ways, important ontological, epistemic, and ethical questions are ignored in support of what has been described so far as cybernetic rationality.

The edges and nodes of new computational diagnoses

In a push to move beyond many of the problems underlying the DSM, programs are currently being refined that can create network maps of symptoms related to certain mental disorders in terms of dynamical systems of data that can be updated over-time. Rather than take symptoms to be the effects of disorders, network models construe diagnoses as the effects of all known relations between corresponding symptoms. In contrast with earlier taxonomies, new network models do not assume some preexisting, latent entity must exist at the basis of a diagnosis. Here, etiology is also brought back into the discussion. As McNally et al. (2015) explain, "[m]ental disorders are best construed as causal systems embodied in networks of functionally interconnected symptoms" (p. 839). Here, individual symptoms of a mental disorder are connected through mereological (part-whole) relationships, signaling a marked shift from the linear causality implied in most biomedical models. In other words, rather than having all symptoms of a mental disorder reduced to one cause, each symptom can in theory serve as a possible cause for any others. As the values and relations (what they refer to as edges) between symptom-nodes change, so do the conceptual contours of the disorders they signify. While such symptom constellations might be framed as topological wholes for pragmatic reasons, each symptom (i.e., node in the network) is never entirely fixed relative to all of the others.

These are modeled on the principles of network theory that has become increasingly popular as of late across many fields of research. With network theory models, a range of variables are mapped as a constellation of nodes, with different styles of lines between them signifying different forms of relationships. Galloway (2004), for instance, describes such network diagrams as fundamental to the general notion of *protocol* on which most information technologies have been built:

> Protocol considers first a network as a set of nodes and edges, dots and lines. The dots may be computers (server, client, or both) ... With this basic "diagram" you can do a number of things.

You can connect the dots—all of them—making a totally connected, distributed network with more than one path to the destination. You can also disconnect dots, even delete dots (no paths, no destination). You can filter out which dots are connected to the network. You can create portals for the addition of future dots. You can designate which kinds of lines you want between the dots (for not all lines are equal; some diverge, flee; others converge, coalesce). In short, a network-as-diagram offers all sorts of possibilities for organization, regulation, and management. (Galloway, 2004, xviii–xix)

This new network paradigm, applied to issues in mental health, constitutes a noteworthy transition from studying disordered individuals to studying observable symptoms and relations between them. The excitement around this approach comes largely from its potential to solve long-standing conceptual problems like whether psychiatric diagnoses differ by categorical type or dimensional degree. Doing away with latent essences underlying each category, researchers hope future interventions might be more effectively tailored to the unique expression of symptoms in each individual case. And while earlier iterations have focused exclusively on observed symptoms and the patterns they form, more recent approaches incorporate non-symptom contributing factors as well.

According to Borsboom (2017), for instance:

> Insofar as factors not encoded in common diagnostic systems play a role (e.g., psychological processes not included in the symptomatology, neural conditions, genetic antecedents), they must do so by: a) constituting the symptom in question (e.g., the symptom of anxiety involves a neural realization in the brain, which partly constitutes that symptom), b) constituting a symptom-symptom connection (e.g., the biological clock is part of the system that generates the insomnia → fatigue relation), or c) acting as a variable in the external field (e.g., chronic pain is likely to be an external factor that causes fatigue). (p. 7)

Borsboom (2017) further differentiates his approach from others because it does not reduce mental disorders to any one systemic scale (e.g., biological or social), as most biomedical models do. Nor does it focus on linear casual mechanisms. As he suggests, such an approach "is perhaps best interpreted as an organizing framework" (p. 11)—akin to Darwin's theory of evolution. And like Darwin's theory, the utility of network frameworks lies in their ability to track non-linear changes in complex systems over time. Here, information collected about the lives of those diagnosed can be input into computer databases to form ever more comprehensive constellations of diagnostic relations (McNally, 2016).

Jones et al. (2017) extend the reach of such models even wider, adding to the possible combinations outlined above any biological, psychological, or social trait not considered a symptom yet having a strong relationship with one or more symptoms. This certainly makes sense if the goal is to account for as many variables and relations between them as possible. And it so happens that technological advancements make mapping massive quantities of variables more feasible than ever before. The long-term goal for such maps is to be employed as clinical tools to either control future behaviors or map patterns of biological, psychological, and social links to which future behaviors are expected to conform (see Jones et al. 2017). Again, this represents a new form of social control that does not rely on discipline directly. Instead, it employs risk assessment techniques to pre-configure behavior, while continuously deferring the possibility of discipline (e.g., involuntary hospitalization) to a later time. Although personal experiences of service users inevitably exert some influence over how such concepts are applied in clinical practice, their effects on treatment are ultimately over-coded by the frame employed by the clinician.

Like earlier neo-Kraepelinian (biomedical) frameworks, new network models of psychopathology highlight key leverage points to intervene on observed causal mechanisms in ways that exert influence over mental activity. Given that we have both the technology (AI) and conceptual tools (information theory) to map more complex patterns of disorder across different scales (e.g., environmental, molecular genetics, etc.), network maps can now more easily trace functional mechanisms well beyond individuals and their brains. However, the ontological gaps described earlier are still latent here, as it is with the RDoC framework referenced above. What is it that such maps ostensibly represent if not the substance of mental disorders or persons themselves? And in terms of ethical implications, what will keep these networks from being repurposed for other goals, like social surveillance? It remains to be seen, for instance, exactly how and where all this information will be stored, protected, and distributed. Unfortunately for service users, such concerns often fall outside the scope of clinicians' expertise.

This has not, however, stopped clinicians and researchers from trying. Such aspirations are embodied in Luxton's (2015) imaginary concept of the "super clinician," an:

> intelligence machine system that would integrate many [digital] technologies ...The system could use facial recognition technology to verify the identity of patients and also advanced sensory technologies to observe and analyze non-verbal behavior such as facial expressions, eye blinking, vocal characteristics, and other patterns of behavior. Computer sensing technology could also assess internal states that are not detectable by the human eye, such as by observing changes in body temperature with infrared cameras or blood flow in the face with high-resolution digital video processing techniques. The system could be capable of accessing and analyzing all data available about patients from electronic medical records, previous testing results, and real-time assessments collected via mobile health devices. (p. 18)

Such an optimistic characterization of how mental health data might be fed into machine-learning technology belies the fact that decisions regarding which variables are meant to signify a symptom and which are not can only be made through negotiations among professionals. Of course, various measures can be written into a protocol that can be programmed to scan-data and read out in a certain way, but such an algorithm will inevitably possess all the biases of its programmer. And given the already poor ethical track record of digital mental health apps to date (Huckvale et al., 2019), there is no shortage of reasons to be concerned about this.

Network theories and other cybernetic approaches have a lot to offer contemporary discussions across clinical psychology and mental health. Yet, there are important ethical—and by extension conceptual—limitations to keep in mind. As computational models are applied more often in health care settings, practices that monitor and record the neurological and physiological activity of those involved in treatment will become increasingly valuable. Here, there will be increasing numbers data sets yielded, providing value for an ever-growing range of private and public interests. An important conceptual problem with proposals such as those in this section, however, is essentially a variation of the ontological gap discussed throughout this book. As Patil and Giordano (2001) explain,

> [p]sychiatric classification requires differentiation between what counts as normality (i.e.- order), and what counts as abnormality

(i.e.- disorder). The distinction(s) between normality and pathology entail assumptions that are often deeply presupposed, manifesting themselves in statements about what mental disorders are.

(p. 1)

Unless alternative ontologies of mental health are developed, new mental health data—collected through apps, mental health notes, AI, or otherwise—will likely remain tethered to emerging markets of medical neoliberalism through the interpretation of and intervention on behaviors construed as symptoms. Despite the way network models provide more options than prior research approaches for mapping complex relations between terms, such maps are nonetheless still flat representations of decontextualized data-points. And insofar as new network models do not rely on methodological individualism, but pharmaceutical interventions do, it is unclear how the former will bridge research to practice other than through a superficial instrumentalism. With such massive amounts of data on symptomatic and non-symptomatic behaviors being collected and networked in real time, it is more imperative than ever to reflect critically on how, and by whom, the boundaries of "mental health systems" are determined, as well as whose practical values are served by mapping mental disorders as if they are reliable constructs.

Note

1 Some portions of this chapter were taken from an earlier publication (Beck, 2020) with permission granted from its publisher, the APA.

5
DISORDER WITHOUT BORDERS[1]

Introduction

In 1992, Deleuze imagined a yet existing system of governance in the form of a highly distributed network of data exchange, where social power is maintained through an automated:

> control mechanism, giving the position of any element within an open environment at any given instant (whether animal in a reserve or human in a corporation, as with an electronic collar) …a city where one would be able to leave one's apartment, one's street, one's neighborhood, thanks to one's (dividual) electronic card that raises a given barrier; but the card could just as easily be rejected on a given day or between certain hours; what counts is not the barrier but the computer that tracks each person's position-licit or illicit -and effects a universal modulation. (p. 7)

Such a scenario, a nascent possibility at the time Deleuze was writing, served to highlight a broader set of concerns he had with the way digital technologies were being coupled with data-collection practices for purposes of surveillance and social control. And yet, it did not take long for this system to become a lived reality for a significant percentage of the world's population.

In 2015, Chinese companies began developing pilots for an experimental social credit system that would be rolled out gradually over the next few years, with it hopefully being nationwide by 2020 (Kostka, 2019). Here, a single score is assigned to each citizen based on criteria ranging from one's buying history and driving record to online behavior. The idea is for such scores to be connected to a specially designed governance structure, shelling out rewards and punishments in ways that would put B.F. Skinner's (2005) *Walden II* to shame. This might be used to determine, for instance, the school a child can get into, the job an adult can get, or where and when a person can travel. While this system of governance is simply the latest version of the hyper-capitalist/communist hybrid society under construction in China for the last several decades, its current form relies uniquely on a digital mass surveillance system that allows citizen's scores to be updated as close as possible to real time. In other words, it relies on cybernetic methods of collecting, circulating, and interpreting data on human behavior and using that data to reorganize the system of governance moving forward.

While China's system might be one of the most overt examples of how a system of surveillance can be coupled with behaviorism for purposes of social engineering, it is certainly not unique in its aims or its approach. With the growing influence of big data monopolies, analogous, albeit more concealed, systems of data collection and surveillance are already operating in full force across American institutions. From his new home in Moscow, Edward Snowden, for instance, continues to pull the curtain back on personal privacy concerns mounting since the passing of the Patriot Act. Companies like Facebook, Amazon, Google, and Microsoft use data about our everyday habits in ways that most people would never be able to fathom, while social institutions ranging from schools to government agencies often partner with these companies in ways that essentially give away data for free. This is closely connected to the concerns about neoliberalism outlined above, insofar as unbridled corporate access to some of the most valuable world resources (i.e., sets of data and the technologies to mobilize them) has created global power imbalances the likes of which the world has never witnessed.

It is important to think critically about relationships between psychology, mental health, and cybernetics not because all psy-practitioners themselves should not be trusted, but because psy-disciplines are situated with broader social and economic systems that have clearly affected how they are organized on nearly every level. Insofar as mental health care has become a multi-billion-dollar, transnational market, it is imperative to understand how such services are shaped through values beyond the health of individuals. Naomi Klein (2008) underscores quite convincingly in her book, the

Shock Doctrine, that the coupling of cybernetics with risk analysis provides the perfect method for expanding capitalism, in the form of neoliberalism, across the globe. Psychologists like Donald Hebb, in fact, played a direct role in this by working with various intelligence agencies to develop mind control techniques that such agencies could apply to group behavior (Klein, 2008). It is thus impossible to trace a comprehensive survey of psy-practices without acknowledging the many ways in which they are have been tailor made for purposes related to social engineering and political control.

This has taken on an unprecedented urgency with the popularization of the internet, and the transformation of mobile devices into data-collection tools. Here, chains of user data are infinitely divisible and replicated for purposes that exist beyond the control of any one individual and/or social group. Clinical researchers have already proposed repurposing portions of this data to map constellations of symptoms for the purposes of shaping human behavior (McNally, 2016). Upstream of this, insurance companies combine this with information they already have to create predictive analytic apps that reduce demand for care professionals (Cosgrove & Karter, 2018). Still further upstream, a handful of data companies, principally Amazon, Google, Microsoft, and Facebook, vie to marketize the world's information and data through ongoing transcription of largely virtual interactions (Beck and Friedman, 2019). Again, the question is not so much whether these uses are right or wrong but, rather, who they benefit and to what broader purposes?

Drawing on the history traced in Chapter 4, therefore, it is important to understand how mental health practices are generally considered successful today only to the extent that they: (1) offer clinical tools for social and communicative control; (2) are no longer connected to any single set of social institutions; and (3) present themselves as pre-packaged and available for application to the concerns of any conceivable ethnic group around the world. It would be something of a misnomer to suggest that Western psychological services reinforce colonial practices because of a series of conceptual errors or a lack of material resources—although these have likely served some roles. But most notably, under the current conditions of transnational capitalist markets, where the economic value of data and information networks rivals that of material goods or services, fruitful overlaps across marketing, data analytics, and diagnostic assessment render decentralized psychological theories most profitable when they operate beyond the control of a handful of institutions.

Going further, this chapter explores how cybernetic frameworks, and the myths of auto-individuation analyzed so far, provide indispensable frames of reference for understanding how psychiatric power has been transformed into the increasingly decentralized network of services of care that exist today. By defining respective concepts of "the individual" in terms of only what can be observed based on the tools, data, and cultural assumptions available at certain moments in time, psy-disciplines can be understood as an evolving network of (first-order) cybernetic technologies in a way that makes their theoretical fragmentation socially meaningful. Thinking about this through the lens of second-order cybernetics, it is important to recognize how interpretations of observed behaviors are always constrained through the frames of reference afforded to the corresponding observer, given their situatedness in history and culture. And yet, as illustrated by the general failure of psychoanalysis, such frames of reference are themselves not always able to be made observable, especially when they are linked to social values that are not acknowledged by the professionals that use them.

Cybernetics, as such, exemplifies what is simply the most recent phase of a historical progression through which technologies of control have been used to support a certain idealized version of social arrangement. Early cybernetic theorists, such as Warren McCulloch (1954) and John von Neumann (1948), gave "voice to [a widely expressed] aspiration to turn a world framed in terms of consciousness and liberal reason into one of control, communication, and rationality" (Halpern, 2015, p. 2). By the same token, Halpern (2015) suggests that their search for a conceptual framework that could "represent thought logically" was, from the start, unavoidably "haunted – animated – by the ongoing problems of organizing [the experience of] time and space inside networks… [such that] the literal mechanisms of thinking [e.g. memory storage and cognitive processing] always haunted computational models" (p. 2). As we move forward, new metaphors for subjectivity are bound to emerge, with the boundaries between oneself and others destined to be reworked into yet imagined forms. Analogous to the ways those like Karen Barad (2007), Donna Haraway (2000), and N. Katherine Hayles (1999) have described cybernetics as reshaping how we think about humanity, therefore, recent applications of cybernetic principles to psychology are yielding new networked forms of subjectivity that will undoubtedly be repurposed for a range of social and economic purposes.

Insofar as mental health services are supposed to be both standardized and tailored to the needs of local geographical contexts, the general notion of boundary management becomes a core value for professionals across psy-fields. Here, boundaries are drawn around groups of individuals (e.g., ethnic groups, nationalities, genders) but also around individuals themselves, separating them from one another. This is often where ideas in cybernetics have been applied most explicitly to the provision of mental health services. Today, boundaries tend to be drawn most often through discourses of risk-management. With biomedical procedures of clinical research, diagnosis, and intervention, mental health service "users" are coded largely in terms of the risks they could pose, as individuals, to others. Risk-assessment discourses not only obscure the extent to which social and/or environmental factors contribute to the severity of symptoms, they also impose arbitrary and normative restrictions (i.e., boundaries) around the modes of expression and types of community diagnosed individuals are able to form with others.

In these ways, biomedical terminology has itself come to provide a heuristic value that connect those seeking treatment to valuable resources in their communities. As Volkmar and Rechow (2013) explain, "[c]ommonality in approaches to classification help us communicate more effectively about clinical problems (rapidly conveying a general sense of the kinds of difficulties exhibited)" (para. 1). And yet, communication is, of course, highly contextual. Even if categories of mental disorder do not represent any set of material conditions accurately, the taxonomic structures they form (e.g., the DSM and ICD) can remain useful to the extent they effectively coordinate action and distribute resources within specific institutional contexts. Insurance companies might request certain diagnoses to justify reimbursement decisions, for instance, while special educators might communicate through them to structure classroom activities. The overarching objective here—beyond merely helping those diagnosed with mental disorders—is thus to more easily categorize aberrant behaviors in terms of already described biomedical symptoms, thereby intervening upon the developmental trajectory of those on the receiving end of services more effectively. It may be most accurate to say simply that mental health diagnoses represent complex processes of social and professional negotiation, which unavoidably structure how symptoms are observed and treated.

As media theorist Alexander Galloway (2004) reminds us, "[y]ou have not sufficiently understood power relationships in [contemporary] society unless you have understood 'how it works' and 'who it works for'" (p. xiii). In other words, if psy-disciplines are held together by a set of historically embedded social technologies, whose interests are such technologies being tailored to and for what broader social purposes? This chapter explores how cybernetics provides a timely set of critical tools to deconstruct global mental health trends while, alternately, serving as the apparatus underpinning these same trends. This is important not only with respect to what a history of cybernetics can add to discussions about the ontological and epistemological statuses of mental disorders but also in terms of what it elucidates about the ethics of data-collection and sharing policies underpinning mental health organizations.

Protocological control and the dividualization of mental health

There have been many different names offered for the every-evolving system of capitalist markets that most people in the world are now living under. *Late-capitalism* has been popular among social theorists. Digital tropes, like *information economy, data-capitalism,* and *surveillance capitalism,* are also common. Then, there is the term *attention economy*, which speaks directly to its links with cognitive neuroscience. And, of course, *neoliberalism* has been in circulation for quite some time. No matter the designation, however, contemporary societies and economic markets have clearly undergone substantial changes over the last few decades. The economic value of data and information networks, for instance, has come to rival that of material goods or services. Fruitful overlaps have emerged across marketing, data analytics, and diagnostic assessment, rendering psychological myths of auto-individuation profitable when they can be circulated beyond the control of a handful of institutions.

In a brief essay about these topics, Deleuze (1992) suggests that a useful lens for emerging modes of social organization is simply *control*. Control societies, as it were, are organized through an increasingly amorphous network of coded regulations, providing continuous feedback to whatever happens to be the source of power. Deleuze distinguishes this relatively new form of social power from the disciplinary societies outlined by Foucault (2003), which were organized primarily through the enactment of laws that, in turn, had to be enforced through arrest, containment, or some other form of physical threat. The speech and thought of bodies living under societies of control, by contrast, are regulated according to a series of highly codified values assigned to them. Such bodies are considered valuable only to the extent their behavioral trajectories, in the form of market predispositions, can be operationalized, monitored, and measured. All of this is expected to conform, moreover, to financial speculations of risk-management employed by competitive local and/or global conglomerates (e.g., corporations, NGOs, non-profits, etc.).

According to Deleuze (1992), the operations underlying control societies are most evident in the new network models of subjectivity emerging, where what used to be "[i]ndividuals have become 'dividuals,' and masses, samples, data, markets, or 'banks'" (Deleuze, 1992, p. 5).[2] In cybernetic terms, *dividuals* can be understood as isolated, mechanistic functions that can be plugged into a range of different systems depending on fluctuations in social value and emerging technical utility. In short, they are data part and parcel of systems of control. The core problem here is no longer discerning what the other knows, but what they desire—a symptom of what mathematician and social theorist Gilles Châtelet (2014) describes, quite aptly, as the obsession with "anticipating the anticipations of others, in singularizing oneself by imitating everyone before everyone else does, in guessing the 'equilibria' that will emerge from cyberpsychodramas played out on a global scale" (p. 133, *emphasis* in original). Here, control is distributed through overarching demands to incessantly compare one's self-worth to others by seeking to understand them even more intimately than one does oneself. This effectively disrupts any sense of temporal continuity between oneself and others, leading to unavoidable paranoia regarding one's status in relation to an imaginary standard (e.g., money).

Integrating Deleuze's (1992) insights with more general ideas from computer science, Galloway (2001) describes the primary mode of organization in control societies simply in terms of *protocols*, which:

> operate at the level of coding: they encode packets of information so that they may be transported, they code documents so that they may be effectively parsed, and they code communication so local devices may effectively communicate with foreign devices. Protocols are highly formal—that is, they encapsulate information inside a technically defined wrapper while remaining relatively indifferent to the content of the information. Protocol is not a synonym for informatization or digitization, or at least not only. While a knowledge of informatization is crucial for understanding the new economy…protocol is something different. It is a distributed management system that allows control to exist within immanent material relations. (p. 83)

In this sense, *protocol=code*. Within contemporary big data repositories, for instance, biomedical information is accumulated on such massive scales that no individual person could ever sift through it all in a single lifetime. And yet, somehow patterns continue to emerge in ways that allow protocols of organizations to continue functioning. As Skott-Myhre (2015) describes:

> The ability to take the massive and potentially genocidal effect of global warming and make it an issue that demands more nuclear plants, hydro-dams and hydrofracking is clear evidence of an abstract system that operates with no regard for living things, whose only purpose is its own expansion and continued existence. (p. 60)

Here, the otherwise human mode of surveillance at the basis of disciplinary control (i.e., the panopticon) has become increasingly digitized, and thus mechanized, such that "[i]nformation flows run along computers and sometimes pass through human beings in order to be transformed into money flow" (Christiaens, 2016, p. 6). The boundaries of dividuals are regulated under societies of control through the non-stop transcription of thoughts, affect, and desire into code that is used to reorganize social institutions in ways that simply produce more code. Protocols undergirding data collection markets, as it were, work directly on the neurological functioning of bodies such that their behaviors can be tracked and shaped more predictably across settings.

In a properly cybernetic form, such societies code an increasing variety of human, and transhuman (Ferrando, 2014), behaviors according to a series of functional relationships between individuals and the objects in their environment. As with the social credit system mentioned above, when humans behave in a manner congruent with expectations set for those objects, their scores go up. When they do the opposite, their scores go down. At some point, one can imagine all processes internal to each human being coded as digital maps of electrico-chemical and physiological networks, with each identified mechanism linked to desirable behaviors that are themselves given a unique score. Given how theories in psychology have been repurposed as social engineering technologies since its inception, it is not difficult to see how myths of auto-individuation (pseudo-AI) play a role in data-centric systems of governance. In this sense, they can likewise be understood as myths of artificial intelligence, since they represent (sometimes successful) attempts to program particular iterations of subjectivity into systems where they did not exist before. They replicate, like viruses, across institutions in ways that have little regard for what was there before.

The concept of the dividual can, in fact, be understood as a logical consequence of the history of auto-individuation myths outlined in Chapter 3.

The transformation of "the individual" from psychoanalysis to behaviorism, then to cognitive neuroscience, overlaps with the emergence of information processing theories and the transcription of all life processes into series of functional mechanisms. Such cyborg semiologies, as Haraway (2000) outlines above, do not merely yield a framework for organic and inorganic substances to be analyzed in analogous terms, they likewise allow parts from one type to be exchanged, at times indiscriminately, for those in the other—all the while maintaining its structure in the same form. Taking a cue from Simondon's general psychology, then, myths of auto-individuation are thus myths exactly because they assume a concept of an individual without accounting for the material processes through which individuation actually occurs. Both the concepts and bodies that come under the control of abstract protocological systems are strictly dividual, insofar as their properties are theoretically indefinite, yet wholly dependent on a particularly arranged series of terms in which they are situated.

Further drawing on Simondon, then, we might say that a dividual emerges in a control society when what might otherwise be considered an "individual body" has become tethered to a specific set of artificial, sociomaterial systems. More specifically, as opposed to enforcing morality through systems of laws and discipline, such societies employ operant condition to link moral codes to the fear of losing something considered essential to one's own existence. Here, affects like fear and anxiety in one area of life are reinforced by linking them either to threats of loss or sadistic pleasure in another. However, because these are only imaginary losses, not actual ones, and pre-individual affect is invested in often contradicting ways, such paranoiac machines render it impossible to secure an "individual identity," as such. This might be experienced as a dissolution of boundaries between self and other—a sense of dissociation from oneself—and as boundaries dissolve, such fear or anxiety can often be especially penetrating. And yet, for Simondon, this is merely a dissolution of certain processes of individuation that have already began.

As virtual participants within contemporary society, it is almost expected that we observe, comment on, and effectively modulate aspects of others' lives that would have previously remained private or completely ignored. Given the quick rise to popularity of social movements like #BlackLivesMatter, Occupy Wall Street, and #Metoo, we can connect this trend, as well, to updates to our general moral code. And yet, any processes of individuation started through these memes break down when various pre-individual affective investments are not able to be sustained past a certain threshold of individuation. At this point, any transindividual links that were previously formed become detached, with the process gradually liquifying until it becomes unrecognizable from what it was.

The problem in societies of control, however, is that protocols are in place that keep such processes of dissolution themselves from reaching conclusion. When pre-individual investments are coded as images of persons or things, they can become captured by the logic of broader socioeconomic markets. Social media platforms, for instance, which operate for tech companies as "market-based systems of interpersonal evaluation" (Curran & Hill, 2017, p. 9), allow users to create reflections of themselves through constellations of sentences, images, and likes that are then fed-back to them as an imaginary set of relations structured through algorithm. Despite the artificial nature of these apparatuses, real feedback loops can nonetheless emerge between processes of dissolution, pre-individual investments, and the protocols of the machine, such that no process—neither individuation nor dissolution—can fully reach completion. All that remains of the body, in this sense, is a series of streams of information, all disconnected, hence its dividualization.

Of course, not all bodies will respond the same to any given machine or set of modulations. Insofar as the behaviors expected to be performed by individual bodies change from one historical epoch to the next, and sociocultural norms vary across geographical location, observed biological differences thus become either more or less adapted to the socioeconomic value system in which they are situated depending largely on each body's interoperability with available technologies. On the one hand, there is a spectrum of artificiality involved here, whereby societies of control must evolve in order to create the appearance of the same. When the explicit rules stop working to enforce the behaviors conventionally associated with them, attempts emerge to codify what was previously able to be enforced implicitly—by insinuating the consequence of transgressions through the punishment of behaviors perceived as opposite to the intended outcome. On the other hand, processes of individuation nonetheless continue to emerge, and not all can be extinguished through existing artificial systems of control.

Such practices are precisely what allow societies of control to continue evolving alongside, while also shaping, human biology. Discipline operates according to a very simple logic. It can only be enacted if someone is caught breaking a law. Then it is enacted immediately, such that the person knows with certainty that they have been disciplined. With control, on the other hand, governance becomes much more complex, and it is this complexity that underlies its success. By combining attention - capturing technology with random number generators, for instance, variable-ratio schedules of conditioning—the same logic at the basis of slot machine—can be automated to ensure that no general pattern in the social logic can be derived. And in this way, the person never knows when or where they might be punished, despite the visualization of it permeated their social sphere. In the ideal version of China's social credit system, there would never need to be a human carrying out orders to punish an individual because an underlying fear will have already been conditioned into the behavior and neurological circuitry of all citizens through persistent imaginary reminders about what happens if the moral code it transgressed. As Deleuze and Guattari (1987) explain, for instance:

> If motorized machines constituted the second age of the technical machine, cybernetic and informational machines form a third age that reconstructs a generalized regime of subjection: recurrent and reversible "humans-machines systems" replace the old nonrecurring and nonreversible relations of subjection between the two elements; the relation between human and machine is based on *internal, mutual communication*, and no longer on usage or action… with automation comes a progressive increase in the proportion of constant capital; we then see a new kind of enslavement: at the same time the work regime changes, surplus value becomes machinic, *and the framework expands to all of society*. It could also be said that a small amount of subjectification took us away from machinic enslavement, but a large amount brings us back to it. (p. 458, *emphasis* in original)

This is a system based essentially on credit, where social values are regulated through a paranoid logic of communicative control. Like the obverse form of a negative theology, the Law is learned through reminders about what not to do. The full boundaries of moral codes, because they include conditions of varying complexity, as described above, are not always able to be made explicit, and the parts that are so cannot be articulated fully—as articulation always presupposes a relation to earlier codes (i.e., precedent), otherwise it risks corruption in meaning. But the face of the authoritative other-subject is never revealed; rather, it remains veiled through symbols of a wholly abstract sense of moral authority, remaining without an obvious, physical embodiment. There are simply rhythms that are felt and/or encoded into narrative form. And yet, all this serves to do is reinforce investment of pre-individual drive in ways that break individuation down before transindividual relations are formed—despite the wealth of information at one's disposal.

Pre-individual investments underlying concepts of mental health

Decades ago, Felix Guattari foreshadowed many of the concerns outlined so far regarding psychiatry and the emerging "mental health industrial complex." From his work as a psychotherapist, he was particularly concerned with how concepts and technologies in psychiatry were being refashioned to support the organization of institutions in ways seemed to ignore those who such institutions were supposed to serve. With this, he described how psy-concepts used within these institutions would often be defined just loosely enough to be applied across entirely different situations, while somehow maintaining enough coherence to function within the day-to-day procedures of those in charge. Analogous to the concept of boundary objects described above, Guattari (2015) refers to such notions, simultaneously useful and abstract, as *institutional objects*, insofar as they facilitate discourse and maintain social expectations within and across professional institutions, despite being ascribed functionally different meanings at different contexts.

Guattari interpreted this concept through a much more psychosocial lens than Star and Greisemer's (1989) did, however. For him, institutional objects are a collective manifestation of Donald Winnicott's (1953) *transitional phenomena*, occupying an "intermediate area of experience…between primary creative activity and projection of what has already been introjected, between primary unawareness of indebtedness and the acknowledgement of indebtedness" (p. 89). Here, there are also obvious corollaries with Freud's theory of affective transference outlined above in Chapter 3. As Eng (2015) explains:

> According to Guattari, when a group fails to become aware of its institutional objects as transitional – when it fails to see the group phantasy in which it participates – it remains hostage to the institutional unconscious, believing that its objects are necessary to its positing of its identity. Its desire, fixed on one object or set of objects that it takes to be sacred and immutable, shackles a group to a single destiny. (p. 456)

Here, it is suggested that all groups have certain principles or assumptions about their work which, despite being unable to be proven, are commonly affixed to their professional identities. At contexts of mental health care, for instance, this is evident whenever diagnoses from the DSM are granted their own agency, apart from the clinical functions they serve. Someone might say something to the extent of "I think he struggles with that because of his ADHD" or "Borderline clients are impossible to work with." Anyone who has worked in mental health settings—perhaps even other human service institutions—has heard such phrases said in a variety of situations. Usually, they are uttered in moments of frustration or confusion; often, this is an attempt to solicit empathy or advice from a co-worker. Nevertheless, this frequent habit grants a social reality—a sense of agency—to a set of categories that research has proven over time to be highly unreliable. At the same time, it grants further legitimacy to those institutions with authority to regulate such discourses.

Beyond its relationship to scientific research or clinical utility, the DSM has become something of a cultural icon with increasing global value. This comes at a time when Western mental health concepts extend across more cultures and contexts around the world than ever before (Dhar, 2019). As explained in more detail in Chapter 4, the use of terms like "service provider" and "service consumer," for instance, illustrates how mental health services have become coded in market terms just as much as clinical, or more specifically, biomedical, ones. Both these phenomena can be read, alternately, as unintended effects of efforts to de-institutionalize mental health services (see Novella, 2010). Many of the care practices that would have, before these movements, been performed exclusively by medical doctors in psychiatric settings are now outsourced, so to speak, to an array of other professionals—like educators, counselors, or social workers. Given the common reliance across many of such professions on notions like "evidence-based" or "data-driven" practice (see Spring, 2007), boundaries otherwise demarcating different institutions involved in care are becoming less and less clear. This is largely because what counts as data across them all is invariably constrained by: (a) what has already occurred, been measured, and stored (i.e., a data archive), and (b) whether new measurements can be translated into digital protocols with relevance to institutional problems (i.e., a cybernetic interface).

Given the amount of data required for these practices, computers and servers are essential to the maintenance of such institutional protocols. The coupling of theses otherwise different social technologies has led to growing optimism. Professionals like McNally (2016), for example, are confident that "[a]dvances in quantitative methods, computational power, and mobile technology will pay if clinical researchers can use idiographic network methods to guide therapeutic intervention in the coming years" (p. 102). And yet, the unbridled excitement about cybernetically networked, data-driven, biomedical care belies growing concerns across nearly every other area of social life concerning the ethical consequences of big data (see Mittelstadt et al., 2016). Today, data of all shapes and sizes represent a potential for profit for those who have access to it and are able to make sense of it in relation to data they already possess. Unfortunately for service users, these concerns generally fall well outside the expertise of clinical mental health workers and even clinical researchers.

Considerations about how data sets about human behavior are collected and stored are, for instance, all but ignored in most proposals for global mental health programs (see Karter & Kamens, 2019). These programs intend explicitly to spread Western models of mental health and disorder even further across the world than they already are. Often, this is packaged with generic phrases like "mental health awareness" or the "world-wide burden of mental illness," with Beach et al. (2016) suggesting, for instance, that a "necessary first step toward reducing the mental and physical health burden imposed by family problems worldwide is to develop a common language about these patterns that allows sharing of information across national boundaries as well as between researchers" (p. 7). And yet, such authors fail to clarify several important dimensions of such a proposal. For instance, who should dictate the rules around how such information will be shared? What, exactly, constitutes a "family problem," or even a "family?" Ostensibly, they grant themselves the authority to narrate such gaps between their data points. This is often where myths of auto-individuation insert themselves into the equation, acting as colonial viruses that decode—or as Deleuze and Guattari (1987) would say, *deterritorialize*—local norms and customs, before overcoding (i.e., reterritorializing) them in terms that can be more easily appropriated by transnational organizations. As with other areas of mental health discourse, such proposals ignore the role of local, social values under the guise of expanding care for more individuals (Dhar, 2019).

With the type of network maps proposed by McNally (2016) and others—outlined in more detail in Chapter 3—what clinical researchers effectively map in the form of biopsychosocial traits are not objects, or really even concepts. Rather, they represent a newly emerging, cybernetic form of institutional objects, as described by Guattari above. Insofar as there is no essence assumed underling any of these constellations, the institutional objects are not exactly diagnoses themselves however, but the network technologies with which new mental health data are collected. In this sense, computational network models serve as expressions of professional value, a form of data-based social currency. They operate effectively as what Pierre Bourdieu (1986) referred to as social capital: "the aggregate of actual or potential resources which are linked to possession of a durable network of more or less institutionalized relationships" (p. 86). Boundaries drawn around mental disorders function as abstract social symbols, which become embedded within circuits (i.e., currents) of movement and are invested with pre-individual affective attachments that cut across different areas of professional and personal life. Such relations are networks of social value in the sense that they: (a) refer to how a certain set of individuals are embedded in proximity to each other and (b) structure what is of significance to certain individuals and dictate this significance is to be expressed. Such relations function similarly as motivators for social practices, which can be made sense of only through meanings that link one set of performed actions (or a series of functional mechanisms) to another.

Deleuze (1992) further characterizes societies of control more generally in terms of a decentralized system of determining value that:

> …marks access to information or rejects it…Perhaps it is money that expresses the distinction between [disciplinary and control societies] best, since discipline always referred back to minted money that locks gold in numerical standard, while control relates to floating rates of exchange, modulated according to a rate established by a set of standard currencies. (p. 5)

In situations where physical discipline is less acceptable and/or not effective, social order can be sustained through a continuous series of modulations, with affect and cognition being linked to normative expectations that are determined primarily by differential categories—like diagnoses, professional identities, or currency—rather than the physical capacities of bodies. Here, psychological myths of auto-individuation operate as constellations of social symbols around which clinical practices and professional protocols are perpetually reorganized. Such frameworks guide the interpretation of new data according to a set of culturally specific, yet often-more broadly useful, assumptions. Once a standard definition of a diagnosis is established and circulated, however, it is sometimes easy to forget how much interpretive flexibility is still built into it for clinical purposes. This is how ideas from psy-disciplines can be applied so seamlessly from one social context to the next (i.e., how they have become decentralized), and how they get used for purposes other than those they were designated for (i.e., clinical ones).

Here, the name of the disorder can be seen through the lens of its utility as opposed to some ideal standard to which it should otherwise conform. Diagnostic categories, as such, function as punctuation marks in mental health narratives, perpetually indexing exceedingly larger scales of social value across social actions and forms of communication. Network constellations, such as the computational models discussed above, can make underlying traces of these movements visible for further empirical analysis or clinical intervention. They map encoded signatures of overlapping brain activity, hormonal adjustments, interpersonal synergies, economic determinants, and patterns of thinking and feeling, which when understood together it becomes the task of those with stakes in clinical treatment to decode through whatever social narratives are available for them. And yet, unlike conventional forms of monetary currency, which have no direct correspondence with anything other than themselves, diagnoses and individual behaviors (e.g., symptoms) are not mutually interchangeable symbols of value.

Any identified behavior—or relation between traits within a constellation of mental health factors—can only be coded as a symptom in terms of its function as a linguistic sign within cultural narratives that transcend clinical contexts. Such signs are not self-referential; they are meaningful only (a) insofar as they link with other signs, signifying something to someone at a certain moment in time, and (b) in relation to other signs, operating across levels of biological, psychological, and/or social arrangement. Exactly what constitutes a symptom (i.e., is defined as a problem) is, as such, constrained by frames of reference that include social, epistemic, and economic investment on the part of mental health service providers and/or clinical researchers as much as those diagnosed. As Simondon would say, these make up the pre-individual affect currents underlying mental health care. If such constellations of value are left unacknowledged in any treatment program, default institutional imperatives to assess risk and control the behaviors of others are likely to dictate why observations at one scale of causal mechanism (e.g., the biological) are afforded greater or less social capital in relation to others. In other words, diagnoses, empty as they are of material substance, become placeholders for the desires of whoever uses them. Insofar as mental health professionals are granted sole authority in determining how diagnoses can be used, it is likely to be their own pre-individual investments that structure treatment rather than those of service users.

Circulating diagnoses as social currency

In best case scenarios, diagnostic categories operate as social heuristics that connect individuals to resources in their environments. Rather than marginalize the culturally relative dimensions of clinical practice, as such, it would prove far more productive to position networks of social value as primary determinants of psychosocial well-being, with diagnoses understood, in turn, as symbols for transferring social capital from one situation to another. In these processes, computational simulations of networks of thoughts, emotions, and behaviors cannot interpret themselves. Network maps, social narratives, and values are necessarily embedded within one another in highly complex ways. All three are also structured largely by what can be observed, which is in turn limited by what observers with authority pay attention to. Insofar as attention is a increasingly valuable commodity under current conditions of capitalism, it is likely to remain constrained by habits of thought that generate the most capital for organizations wielding the most social power.

Before categories of mental disorder are imported even further across national borders with data about them circulated across an even greater variety of social institutions, it is imperative for those involved in such procedures to reflect critically on what exactly diagnoses are meant to signify and whether they can successfully support the sociocultural values unique to each local context in which the can now be found. It is promising that a wealth of critical research has already emerged in response to such Global Mental Health movements. Bhargavi Davar (2014), for instance, has criticized them as well as other abstract concerns about the "burden of mental disorders," describing them as extensions of earlier colonial projects to impose Western cultural norms unto Indian communities. China Mills (2014) speaks similarly about the danger of "diagnostic creep," where a greater variety of experiences worldwide are being encoded into psychiatric terms. Kirmayer and Pederson (2014) caution that such trends have unwittingly shifted the focus away from important structural (i.e., socioeconomic) issues that are so often at the root of psychological suffering, especially in what tends to be referred to as the "global South."

To imagine an alternative to the colonial impulses underpinning global mental health movements (see Dhar, 2019), a conceptual shift is required away from categorizing mental disorders in terms of deviant individual behaviors, toward thinking about how they are expressed in-between social actors participating in culturally bound practices. Within such practices, diagnoses trace boundaries around historically situated networks of social and professional value.

Not only do such categories function symbolically to connect individuals to necessary social resources, but, like forms of currency, their circulation across time and space can be mapped to analyze fluctuations throughout broader social networks (i.e., markets). Given the privileged social value of information and data within our increasingly global economic system, thinking about diagnoses as social currency likewise invokes ethical issues beyond the epistemological and ontological statuses of mental disorder—like the ethics of data-collection and other neoliberal social trends.

It is likewise important to recognize, and appreciate, the extent to which diagnoses are used outside of professional contexts today, for a wide range of social and political purposes. Receiving a diagnosis like ASD invariably produces a series of material effects beyond the extent to which certain resources are made either more or less available for a particular person or family. It also reframes how individuals who are diagnosed are perceived by others in the world more generally in a way that could alter how they are able to navigate their environment and hence sustain any sense of livelihood. As Woods (2017) explains, in this way, processes of diagnosis form "looping effects" between individuals, terms, and social institutions in ways that influence diagnosed persons well beyond clinical treatment.

This is also the sense in which diagnostic terms like autism can function as forms of social identity, comparable to other culturally specific identifiers including race, sexual orientation, or gender. Willey (2006) refers, for example, to the "Aspie question" of whether or not to "come out" as having Asperger Syndrome (AS): "if you choose to tell about your AS, you will run the risk of others having reservations and doubts about your abilities and maybe ever your personality on the whole" (p. 30). Groups like the neurodiversity movement, for instance, have reinterpreted diagnostic terms like "Autism" specifically as a form of *neurodivergent identity* that signifies to one another certain collective anxieties as well as liberatory desires towards a new mode of living together (Kapp et al., 2013). Such loosely defined factions engage critically with biomedical characterizations of autism, often opting instead for social disability approaches to autism and other traits associated with neurodevelopmental disorder. Here, most prefer identity first language (i.e. "I am Autistic") as opposed to person first language (i.e., "I am a person with autism"), with the latter taken as a sign that autism is something that can be removed from a person.

Nick Walker (2014), a popular autistic academic, researcher, and blogger, breaks the concept of neurodiversity down even further, distinguishing between the following three meanings of the term:

> Neurodiversity is a biological fact. It's **not** a perspective, an approach, a belief, a political position, or a paradigm. That's the **neurodiversity paradigm** (see below), not neurodiversity itself.
>
> Neurodiversity is **not** a political or social activist movement. That's the **Neurodiversity Movement** (see below), not neurodiversity itself.
>
> Neurodiversity is not a trait that any individual possesses. Diversity is a trait possessed by a group, not an individual. When an individual diverges from the dominant societal standards of "normal" neurocognitive functioning, they don't "have neurodiversity," they're **neurodivergent** (see below). (p. 6–9)

While such ideas started circulating during the early 2000s through online forums and websites for what Blume (1998) referred to then as "high-functioning autistics," they have more recently become transformed, and at times appropriated, through a range of different initiatives across clinical settings and those like schools and industry. Companies promoting values like "Neurodiversity in the workplace" (Molko, 2018), for instance, while certainly providing valuable opportunities to individuals who would not otherwise have them, nonetheless take a term that was inherently subversive and appropriate it for their own economic reasons. As Remington (2015) describes,

> Microsoft has announced its intention to hire more autistic people – not as a charitable enterprise but because, as corporate vice-president Mary Ellen Smith said: "People with autism bring strengths that we need at Microsoft." Employing autistic people makes good business sense. (para. 1)

The meaning of "neurodiversity" is clearly different across these two groups—the neurodiversity movement and Microsoft. Both use the term to express their own pre-individual investments, connecting it to a certain group dynamic they consider beneficial to their respective projects. Likewise, both operate outside of any pre-individual investments on the part of clinical researchers and mental health professionals. What was previously a clinical category to help clinicians do their jobs, in order words, has come to operate as exchange currency for pre-individual affect, as much as for money or material resources, for a range of different interest groups. While there might have been a point in the history of psychiatry that behaviors associated with mental disorders were considered risks to only the most established social institutions, today it appears more accurate to say that data on mental disorders and the technologies associated with them increasingly represent socioeconomic commodities that can be attached to a much broader range of risks across diverse cultures and economic markets.

The population of those labeled with any given psychiatric pathology is as diverse as any other group of individuals, and yet, those within such groups often share styles of deviation from social norms in ways that create value for not only themselves but a range of others as well. In any case, attempts to define a group of individuals primarily according to the risks they might pose to others, or even oneself, merely reinforces a logic of exclusion that places arbitrary constraints on the platforms through which those with notable neurological variations might amplify or otherwise modulate their desires, as well as their capacities to feel and sense their worlds. As outlined in more detail in Chapter 6, it is often only at the unpredictable junctions between thought, affect, and sensation that such bodies, given their idiosyncratic forms of expression, can interact creatively with available technologies and conceptual schemas that would otherwise be managed for them.

Notes

1 Some portions of this chapter were taken from an earlier publication (Beck, 2020) with permission granted from its publisher, the APA.
2 Anthropologists understand "the dividual…to be thoroughly embedded, and inextricably engaged, in relationships with particular places and particular others—and yet in the immediate interactions of changing situations the person is understood to change in accordance with movements through places and relationships" (Smith, 2012, p. 53). In the sense used by Deleuze, however, "the dividual… [is] a physically embodied human subject that is endlessly divisible and reducible to data representations via the modern technologies of control, like computer-based systems" (Williams, 2005, para. 4).

6
THE NETWORK AS A MODE OF BEING

Introduction

Throughout this book, the concept of psychological myths of auto-individuation has been used to diagnose a historical trend in the overlapping histories of cybernetics, psychology, and mental health care. With each history outlined above, a set of relations between tools, concepts, and social contexts, that were previously invisible, are revealed through narratives that render them socially valuable. Each myth of auto-individuation likewise is wrapped around an ideal image of "an individual," without accounting for the material conditions through which individuation, as described by Simondon, occurs. And yet, this illustrates, simultaneously, psychology's social and historical embeddedness as well as its general social utility. There is a remarkable adaptability underpinning many theories in psychology, whereby they can quickly evolve as social conditions provide new technical metaphors. Whether this is because of "physics envy" or a general concern for the value of their own discipline, psychologists have been quick to repackage old ideas by linking them to flashy new gadgets (e.g., switchboard circuits and brain-imaging technology), creating useful social technologies in the process. Today, the most powerful tools in general are clearly information-based, and we see that, in many ways, psychology was ahead of the curve on this point. And yet, when it comes to social networks and the function data serves within them, psychologists are late to the party.

What would it take to chart an alternative to the highly institutionalized thought (i.e., information) processes underpinning societies of control? This book has argued for a conceptual shift that moves beyond mapping constellations of individual symptoms or neural activity as if they each constituted first-order cybernetic systems. Instead, diagnoses have been described as certain modes of expression of historically situated, collective anxieties. Mental disorders, here, operate as signs that can be read variably depending on what is considered valuable in whatever context they are invoked. Narratives and network maps initiate social change, as it were, only if they are considered valuable in the communities where they are made available for use. *If* cybernetics can play a useful role in such processes, it is necessary to engage with concepts of "mental health" with a critical reflexivity that decodes social values and narratives conventionally underpinning "treatment" (see Johnstone & Boyle et al., 2018). Going even further, however, there must be a recognition of the latent social power inhering in liminal spaces between cultural narratives, network maps, and digital technology. This is precisely where new social ecologies are most likely to emerge in formations that can successfully counter the contemporary exigencies of mental health, beyond the constraints imposed by totalizing drives of today's data-driven capitalism.

The title of this chapter, *The network as a mode of being*, refers to the name that Fernand Deligny (2015), an experimental educator, activist, writer, and filmmaker, gave to the development and maintenance of collective living spaces for outcast youths he contributed to in France throughout the 1960s and 1970s. On a small piece of property in the Cévennes region, adults and children who had been labeled, for various reasons, "socially delinquent," often "autistic," and in some cases "non-verbal," lived alongside each other and worked together to sustain their network in whatever ways they could. Despite the professional mental health background of some adults there, they did not rely on organized programs of clinical intervention, or even explicitly defined outcomes set in advance for their daily activities. Their general refusal to rely on preconfigured diagnostic taxonomies or established clinical techniques stemmed from a desire to avoid charting relations between one another according to already constructed social expectations, which would likely have been irrelevant to the embodied and locally situated dimensions of their evolving lived practices. The underlying mission, rather, was to provide a place where the children living there could express their impulses without fear of judgement or retaliation, which they were likely used to receiving based on the state of the youth mental health care system in France at the time.

For this collective to subsist, it was imperative that everybody living there did what they could each day to ensure basic needs were accounted for. Here, daily activities around cooking and maintaining the property as well as the organization of living spaces were kept intentionally routine, and yet persistent exploration of the landscape was encouraged in an almost ritualized fashion. Many of the children who lived there would likely be diagnosed with ASD today, if they were still alive (Hilton, 2015). But there, their behaviors were not framed in terms problems the adults were expected to solve. As Deligny (2015) explains, "[t]o respect the autistic being is not to respect the being that he or she would be as other," (i.e., represented as another in terms of how they are referenced), but simply "to do what is needed so the network can weave itself" (p. 111). Here, Deligny contrasts the "humans that we are," which are the humans we imagine and symbolize ourselves to be, with a mode of being together networked through a common social body that presents new capacities for affect and action for those participating in its persistent reorganization.[1]

Perhaps most impressive about these experiments, then, is simply how long they were able to provide sustained care to children who would have otherwise been institutionalized, while remaining outside of mainstream funding streams and using a set of tools that were crafted without explicit reference to other clinical settings. As Damian Milton (2016) explains, "[s]everal decades before the growth of the neurodiversity movement, Deligny and his collaborators were rejecting notions of autism as a pathological deviation from the norm, and instead were," quoting Deligny (2015), "… in search of a practice that would exclude from the outset interpretations referring to some code; we did not take the children's way of being as scrambled, coded messages addressed to us" (Deligny, 2015, p. 79). A wealth of detailed notes and several noteworthy films remain from these experiments in social care, providing, at the very least, a trace of the network logic undergirding their collective practices. Perhaps the most impressive set of records is the extensive assortment of maps—imprints of movements (they referred to them as wander lines) enacted between those who lived there. Such maps were created by the adults there and collected over a span of several years. For hours each day, one of the adults would follow the movements of everyone in a room, tracing overlapping lines between designated areas and marking any points of significance. In a very real sense, these lines were considered expressions of the network itself, imprinted by a logic of the arrangement of bodies and objects as they related to one another other across time and space.

Deligny's project in general serves as possible case study highlighting what and approach to care that prioritizes networks of living as opposed to artificial networks of meaning might look like. It also offers a concept of the network that is not modeled on digital technologies and yet can be used to analyze how social relationships are maintained through them. As such, it offers an excellent example of what Guattari (1995) refers to as a *post-media* ecology, illustrating how:

> [t]echnological developments together with social experimentation in these new domains are perhaps capable of leading us out of the current period of oppression and into a post-media era characterised by the reappropriation and resingularisation of the use of media. (p. 5)

As outlined above, the history of psychology is essentially a history of digital mediation based on various *frames* of the individual. Through most mental health programs' general reliance on the DSM, they have come to operate in similarly mediated ways. This is not the way Deligny's maps were used, however. According to Ogilvie (2013), while they were certainly a type of technology, as well as a form of social experimentation, they were not a method of "x-raying 'objects' of experience, but of giving shape to the encounter between living beings who, although they are not subjects, are presences whose truth can reveal themselves as forms" (p. 413). Rather than being deployed to interpret and condition the behaviors of the children, the maps served as visual starting points for the adults during what served loosely as group supervision sessions, where they learned gradually deconstruct their expectations of the children and redirect their attention to the entire network of relations—including, at the very least, the thoughts, affects, and behaviors of both the adults and children living there, which is different than their minds or brains. Deligny (2015) adds:

> I shall say the same thing about the mode of being in a network, which is perhaps the very nature of human beings, 'the mind' merely intervening into the bargain, in this case, and its work is the excess rather than the structure of the network. (p. 40)

Lived social networks (including programs of research and mental health) are organized through processes that cannot be represented in their entirety. In each instance of social interaction, there are essential elements to how representations are brought together that, by their very natures, must remain implicit within the modes of interaction as they are enacted.

When it comes to mental health services, therefore, something more than deinstitutionalization or decentralization is required to develop spaces outside of the professionalization and medicalization permeating most organizations today. Perhaps the criteria for abnormality in any given case should also be decentralized and linked directly to the resource needs of local communities, rather than simply encoded as problems with individual behaviors. Beyond analyses of social risk and reward, cultural artifacts would be created in ways that facilitate ongoing collective arrangements where processes of individuation are cultivated. With this, deinstitutionalized care would have to extend beyond the scopes of particular individuals, to include social networks constitutive of the thoughts and communication habits common across mental health professionals and psychological researchers. In other words, it is imperative that ideas and assumptions related to "mental health" in general be deinstitutionalized, in addition to the distribution of local resources.

This underscores the protocological limits of "edge" and "node" models of representation like those used in the network maps outlined in Chapter 3. The primary omissions from this logic are social value pre-individual fields, and collective desire. Sure, data about names given to thoughts and maybe even emotions can be collected with these models. Categories of social relationship can be created that correspond to certain nodes. But affect, in the way that it is experienced in relation to others, is something that exceeds the representational capacities of any diagnostic tool. Here, affects are chaotic elements, "noise," eluding processes of observation and cognition more generally. This is why Simondon considered our contemporary technical mentality "incomplete and in conflict with itself in the domain of the affective categories, because it has not yet properly emerged" (p. 1). By his account, this places humanity in the position of slave to their technologies precisely because they are treated as "other" from themselves.

Psychoanalysis, behaviorism, and cognitive neuroscience each provide a unique mytho-theoretical framework that allows those who employ their technologies to see relationships between objects and bodies that would otherwise be invisible (or perhaps non-existent). Biomedical models similarly illustrate certain humans as inherently more at-risk or likely to pose risks than others, based on characteristics that cannot be seen without their tools. It is simply not possible, however, to see *all* relationships *all* the time. Different theoretical frameworks, while also useful for something somewhere, cannot be combined into a universal framework. Attempts to do so are effectively what lead to paranoia by trapping individual cognition in a world divorced from transindividual affect. The question becomes, therefore, why should anyone pay attention to a certain set of relationships as opposed to others?

Deligny's concept of the network as a mode of being demonstrates something important here, as well. The maps they created had no meaning outside of (a) the evolving collective out of which they were created and (b) the group sessions in which they served as critical deconstructive tools. Such maps were not simply coded representations of data that were subsequently matched with other data sets so that a general set of networks could be developed and used to interpret the meaning of children's behaviors on later dates. It is only in the abstraction—through digitalization, perhaps—from a living network of collective relations to an imaginary, or at least symbolic, system, that affective processes can become severed from cognitive ones. This is also how specific technologies become permanently linked with specific individuals (e.g., as a profession) for the purpose of sustaining an artificial system of code (e.g., capitalism).

The previous chapters highlighted several different histories that reveal essential overlaps across psychology and cybernetics. They likewise provide a series of case studies for some ways cybernetic frameworks—the theoretical bedrock of contemporary computer and information sciences—have become entrenched intractably within the practices and protocols of, not only the biomedical industrial complex, but any network of social organization that relies on financial resources for its survival. Although capitalism is a global force, there is at least one notable limit to the way systems of mental health care that have so far been structured by it: collective advocacy organized over the internet. To define any set of individuals primarily according to the financial risks they might pose to others, or even oneself, reinforces a logic of exclusion, placing arbitrary constraint on the platforms through which those with notable neurological variations might express themselves. And yet, it is often only at the edges of society that such bodies, given their idiosyncratic forms of expression, can interact creatively with available technologies, and the data associated it with, that would otherwise be managed for them. It is here that, as described by Guattari (1995), "the inventiveness of treatment distances us from scientific paradigms and brings us closer to an ethico-aesthetic paradigm" (pp. 8–9), and as Deleuze (2007), drawing on Spinoza, so aptly reminds us: "we prattle on about the soul and the mind…but we don't know what a body can do" (para. 33).

The techno-politics of hacking

The metaphor of "the hacker," as someone who transgresses social boundaries, is a popular—if perhaps played-out—figure within online cultures and circles of critical theorists. In popular media, by contrast, hackers tend to be portrayed either as highly skilled criminals who anonymously infiltrate government systems or 40-year-old men who isolate themselves in their parents' basement. In her essay on the hacktivist group Anonymous, Gabriella Coleman (2011) cautions against such worn-out tropes, instead defining various collectives of self-identified "Geeks and hackers" simply according to their overlapping desires to:

> build and configure technology at work and for fun, communicate and collaborate copiously with one another using these technologies, and, most significant, derive and express deep pleasure and forms of value by inhabiting technology. These experiences shape and yet do not simplistically determine their publics, their politics, and their ethical commitments, especially since hackers do not exist in isolation but are deeply entangled in various distinct institutional and cultural webs and economic processes. (p. 515)

There is an inherent playfulness to the social character of "the hacker," which transcends the use of digital technology even though this link has become so concretized in public consciousness. In this sense, the hacker is a digital substitute for "the trickster," the classic cultural archetype that exposes the limits of conventional wisdom by embodying precisely that which such wisdom seeks to conceal.

As Coleman (2012) further elaborates:

> As part of this practical capacity, the very nature of hacking — turning a system against itself — is the process of using existing code, comments, and technology for more than what their original authors intended. This is the paradox of constraint. Since many technical objects are simultaneously bound by certain limits yet exhibit potential excesses (Star & Griesemer 1989), during the course of their existence, they can be exploited and redirected toward new paths of functionality by acts of hacking. (p. 98)

The hacker is relevant to the concerns of the current book for several reasons. The above tropes aside, hackers often occupy positions at the edges of society. This might start, for instance, by developing an interest in certain machines that few around such individuals understand. Whether they are made to feel strange because of this interest or develop this interest because they are made to feel strange, it can turn into a passion; at some point, it might even become a marketable skill. What is most important for the hacker, however, is not that this skill aligns with some standard social value, but that it can be expressed creatively in ways that connect them with others who possess similar capacities for socio-technical expression.

Guattari (1996) describes, for instance, how "information and communication machines do not merely convey representational contents, but also contribute to the fabrication of new assemblages of enunciation, individual or collective" (p. 96). The collective assemblage of enunciation he references is neither a State nor an already constituted social institution; it is a certain style of network formed with others based the expression of affect, thought, and technical ability. Taking a cue from Simondon (2007), hacking can thus be framed as a particular mode of collective activity that mediates between the technical and the aesthetic, on one hand, and the pre-individual and the transindividual, on the other. In these liminal spaces, technologies are transformed in the moments that affective currents linking them to processes of individuation reach a previously established threshold, thus crystalizing into a new metastable state.

To fully understand the hacker, then, it is also necessary to understand the inherently sociopolitical nature of the internet. The internet is *not* an object, but it is also not a subject. Neither does it mediate between a group of subjects and a group of objects. If anything, the internet is an evolving ecosystem of emergent cultures and information—a digital ecosphere of unconscious psychic material, ranging from socially repressed emotional content to liberated desire. Endless sequences of symbols, images, videos, and otherwise random movement are encoded and decoded through though endless sequences of 1s and 0s, as if these were two parallel processes of the same infinite universe. Rather than simply getting lost in the many different streams of information constituting media, hackers focus on what the technical relations underlying code make possible for specific social groups. It is not simply being able to read code or type it in the right order that matters; the trick lies in reading it for what is not immediately there.

According to Coleman (2012), again:

> Hackers are thus attuned not simply to the workings of technology but also seek such an intimate understanding of technology's capabilities and constraints that they are positioned to redirect it to some new, largely unforeseen plane. They collectively and individually derive pleasure in outwitting constraint. In essence, while hacking follows a craftlike practice, it is predicated on a stance of craftiness to move the craft forward. Hacking is where craft and craftiness converge. (p. 98)

This is effectively a deconstruction of Freud's prioritization of repressive substitution as a mode of analogical mediation. The logic underpinning any act of hacking is quite simple and can be understood according to the following formula: disorder in the program → indeterminacy in the protocol → an opportunity to hack. This applies as much to technical as to social problems, and it is what makes hacking such an unavoidably political endeavor. Elaborating further, Coleman (2011) notes the way "free software developers have come to conceptualize the underlying directions of software, source code, as an example of free speech and have devised legal instruments to ensure this code remains accessible for viewing, modifying, and circulating" (p. 513). This is especially relevant given the concerns overviewed above regarding how data is treated as a commodity under contemporary capitalism. Here, data itself becomes a tool that can be used for a wide range purposes, some of which contribute to corporate growth while others create opportunities for more distributed resource sharing practices (see Kostakis & Bauwens, 2014).

As outlined throughout this book so far, the sociotechnical apparatuses undergirding such ecospheres are steadily becoming transformed in the ways they are applied to new problems alongside other technologies—specifically those from psychology. The overarching goal of those with authority under control societies is to "produce the world as an interface, making attention itself a material and scalable technology" (Halpern, 2015, p. 85). It is thus not in their interest for information technologies be made widely available for fair and open use. In accordance with conventional neoliberal values, those with the resources to *pay* attention to and understand these changes stand to benefit from them the most. And yet, the ways in which protocols are written into information technologies often restrict their use to only those purposes envisioned by their creators. Often, this involves collecting data on every aspect of each user's life to improve upon such protocols in ways the further these same attention capturing purposes.

Hacking constitutes a direct affront to such authorial voices, insofar as it infringes on their abilities to generate income. In this sense, hacking represents a risk, which is why data-security is such a booming industry. As Mirowksi (2015) describes, the growing network of bio-psycho-social data discussed throughout this book effectively renders capitalist "markets… the greatest information processor [ever] known" (p. 11). Here, information and financial markets are forged into common frameworks through a heightened use of risk-analysis technology over conventional disciplinary methods essential to Fordist processes of production—as outlined by classical-liberal economic theory (see Smith, 1982). Insofar as mental health services are dependent on financial resources (i.e., capital), it is likely, in turn, that economic risk assessment will continue to control how, where, and to whom such services are provided.

Identifying the glitches in mental health programs

By now, the ways in which mental health care has become re-configured since deinstitutionalization, in the form of a highly bureaucratic version of human resource management, should be obvious. What should also be obvious are the ways in which earlier cybernetic programs planted many of the seeds for this broad transformation of service to occur. As Halpern (2015) explains, Wiener was an early proponent of the idea that "human behavior could be mathematically modeled and predicted, particularly under stress; thereby articulating a new belief that both machines and humans could speak the same language of mathematics" (p. 43). It did not take long for cybernetic models in this vein to be extended to theories about mental health and disorder, whereby "[c]ommunication failure was, in [Wiener's] terms, the analogue to mental illness" (p. 67). Psychiatric diagnoses have thus come to be reframed under cybernetic models in terms like "diseases of memory" or problems with "executive functioning," reducing a complex range of daily life issues to mechanistic, functional problems—e.g., a lack of "storage space" or "neurotransmitter interference" (p. 67). As outlined so far throughout this book, such metaphors have come to be circulated as fact, rather than heuristic, across a broad range of social institutions, often under the generic banner of 'mental health.'

And yet, it is possible that the popularly noted increase in developmental disorders around the world (see Wazana et al., 2007) could signify something beyond growing degrees of variation in the development of individual brains. Even if brains are, in fact, changing (as they always do), higher rates of neurodevelopmental diagnoses could be read alternately as a symptom of various viscerally felt gaps in what we think we know about humans and their brains, based on the data-archives and myths of auto-individuation at our disposal. In societies of control, the socioeconomic values assigned to ostensibly disparate social institutions (e.g., families, schools, health organizations, governments, etc.) are continually reorganized to conceal what they cannot prove to be true, with biomedical theories of subjectivity facilitating this concealment. Cybernetics has been marketed from the beginning as "a science of control or prediction of future events and actions" (Halpern, 2015, p. 25). It is only because cybernetics tends to be used for purposes like probability assessment and communicative control, however, as opposed to conceptual consistency, or even truth, that it can effectively regulate human behavior in terms of a "black box" model where anything not relevant to the observer's purposes are ignored.

As a conceptual case in point, consider an example based on Claude Shannon's (1971) *Mathematical Theory of Communication*: a common pair of ideas used together often across whatever boundaries still exist between neuroscience (Schmidt et al., 2013), electrical engineering (Shannon, 1971), and computer science (Unger, 1995): race conditions and logic gates. These concepts represent a certain type of problem that emerges whenever there are material conditions under which invalid executions, or any unanticipated activity, in general, emerges at junctures where multiple information pathways "race" toward a shared information output gate. Among any set of (a) neurotransmitters in a brain, (b) DNA regulated protein sequences, or (c) input pathways in a computer or electrical system, an array of 'glitches' can be observed under such race conditions denoting either a temporary disruption in the general flow of information or, in extreme cases, permanent alterations in the functions of the inputs as they were initially encoded.

Notably, the precise extent to which any set of race conditions might affect the overall functionality of a given program is never able to be known in advance with enough certainty to be fixed with any degree of permanence. In the context of computer programming, code with high-risk race conditions is to be avoided whenever possible, while various solutions are invented and circulated amongst users of programs in which glitches have occurred so that they can be more easily patched in the future. With neuroscience, on the other hand, the goals of studying such circumstances are often tied to the development of a biological interventions that might inhibit momentary breakdowns in neural communication—or at least keep the effects of any unanticipated behaviors to a minimum. And yet, for those who desire a perfectly, still unrealized, cybernetically linked world, the performance of brains and computers would interface in manners allowing for "glitches" in either to be fixed according to analogous technological platforms or circuit diagrams.

The application of such cybernetic metaphors are common throughout the literature on human development. According to a study by Klin et al. (2009), for instance, during the first few years of life those who meet current diagnostic criteria for ASD appear to lack a general preference—ostensibly present in most individuals—for biological (i.e., social) movement over other perceptible stimuli in their environment. The authors describe how "[b]y two-years-of-age…children [identified with autism] are on a substantially different developmental course" than their neurotypical counterparts, "having learned already from a world in which the physical contingencies of coincident light and sound are quantifiably more salient than the rich social information imparted by biological motion" (p. 260). As a result, 'information' from the environment that would otherwise be filtered out by the attentional processes of most children can at times be focused on quite intently by those who meet criteria for ASD. Autistic people themselves have described this in terms like "sensory overload," with various self-stimulatory (stimming) behaviors often attributed to such experiences. And yet, within a neurodiversity paradigm, this variation in human development predisposes such children to forms of embodied desire that are often expressed through an intimacy with tools and objects (i.e., restricted or repetitive behaviors) that make others uncomfortable, despite feeling natural to them. Drawing on Malabou (2012), the question for those across all spectrums of neurodiversity is thus, again, "what do we do with our brains?"

This is where cultures (i.e., social networks) can play an essential role in how neurodiversity is expressed. According to Guattari (1995), ontogenetic development is most dynamic during the early phase of development in what he describes as the *cultural unconscious*. During this time, a range of affective capacities and rhythmic modulations of expression are incorporated into one's embodied comportment, such that simultaneously more stable and more complex patterns of behaviors can emerge over time. In the words of developmental psychologist Esther Thelen (1985), "such fundamental coordinative structures…encode certain constrained muscle combinations and as a consequence of their organization, a fundamental timing property" (p. 227). While behaviors learned later on in life—for instance, those that might be more properly described in terms of social interaction or communication—are not determined entirely by the pre-individual gestures linked together during this phase, the structural repertoire of known behavioral variations indexed for subsequent encounters with others nonetheless becomes highly associated with the bio, psycho, and social rhythms synchronized through such structural constraints.

And yet, unexpected actions are always possible regardless of the degree of stereotypy expressed up to any given point. To borrow a concept from mathematical chaos theory, for instance, "if you have two sets of initial conditions, or two points in phase space, extremely close to each other, the two ensuing trajectories, though close to each other at the beginning, will eventually diverge exponentially away from each other" (Baranger, 2001, p. 6). Given any two proximally defined systems (e.g., human bodies or neuronal assemblies), however coordinated they appear at a given moment in time, they will over time continue to diverge from one another unless an overarching infrastructure is in place whereby any unanticipated movements can be deterred, with only those deemed necessary for boundary maintenance to be maintained.

Such organizational gatekeeping procedures allow for the interpretations of risk represented at overriding scales of influence to effectively dictate the response protocols, or even boundary object implementation, elsewhere in the infrastructure. While a structural hierarchy might temporarily emerge integrating representations of possible action for members operating at each of the different scales, any underlying biopsychosocial rhythms supporting it can remain coordinated only insofar as the interpretations and representations (i.e., codes) of risk granted broadest organizational authority correspond with sequences of behavior (i.e., protocols) that effectively maintain proper functioning across the bulk of the networked systems.

Depending on whether or not a child feels supported in their environment, for instance, they might become comfortable expressing themselves idiosyncratically through their natural intimacy with objects, or, to the contrary, they might be artificially conditioned to replicate socially normative behaviors for the pleasure of those around them.

This effectively constitutes Michelle Dawson's (2004) critique of aversion therapies such as those used conventionally in *applied behavioral analysis* (ABA), for instance. In her piece titled *The Misbehaviour of Behaviourists*, she describes, for instance, how certain set of programs of behavioral intervention carried out on children in the 1970s was deemed warranted by researchers at UCLA largely on the basis that:

> the children's disordered behaviours caused emotional distress in their parents; the behaviours were disruptive and judged unacceptable by society and the children's peers; the behaviours also displaced the proper functioning of these children, who were said to be suffering; and [therefore] intervention at the earliest possible sign of deviant behaviours was necessary since the prognosis for adolescence and adulthood was notoriously poor and treatment later in life was known to be futile (para. 21)

This program came to be referred to as the "Feminine Boy Project," since its organizers applied behavioral principles like punishment and negative reinforcement to altering certain behaviors exhibited by young boys who were considered by their parents to be overly feminine. Similar aversive techniques have since been applied in other cases to behaviors labeled "autistic" in attempt to replace them with more "socially appropriate" ones. This is, of course, Skinner's myth of operant-individuation applied to child therapy. Here, complex systems of rewards and punishments are structured to elicit and reinforce a predetermined social behavior or generalize a set of behaviors from one context to another. And yet, very few ever stop these procedures to question what such behaviors express for the bodies performing them, bodies which are always unique in their ability to be affected and affect others in the world. Instead, the values of such behaviors are effectively reduced to a series of functional variables that can be modulated according to the overarching goals tied to whatever social environments the child is forced to navigate.[2]

One of the most concerning current examples of this approach to "treatment" is the Judge Rotenberg Center, "a self-described residential school and treatment center" in Massachusetts, where minors have consistently reported administrations of painful shock treatments in the form of a Graduated Electronic Decelerator (GED) for similar behavioral shaping reasons. According to Neumeier and Brown (2020)—two autistic activists who are actively working to have the center closed—whereas residents of the center were traditionally individuals with developmental disabilities, the population has shifted recently to include growing numbers of individuals with DSM diagnoses who were referred to them from the criminal justice system. The GED techniques the center implements can be attributed directly to "a protégé of infamous behaviorist B.F. Skinner who wanted to bring his mentor's fictional behaviorist utopia Walden II to life but needed a captive audience to do it" (p. 196). Going further, they describe recurring PTSD reported by many former residents, two of whom testified about their experiences during a public FDA hearing about whether the center should be permanently closed. Despite their testimony, a series of legal battles ensued following the hearing that ultimately allowed the center to continue using GED for ABA.

Upon looking more closely at the demographics, however, an even more complicated picture emerges. According to Neumeier and Brown (2020), "in the 2015–2016 school year, JRC's school age population was 81.5% Black or Latinx people, with all categories of people of color or racial minorities combined comprising 87.4% of its population" (p. 199). They further describe the ongoing existence of the JRC as an extension of the prison industrial complex overcoded in 'mental health' terminology. It requires a very strange myth of auto-individuation indeed for normal human development to be reduced to a series of events whereby a person learns what is right or wrong by associating it with either fear or a treat response, which is in turn somehow supposed to shape them to be a "normal," "healthy," or generally "happy" person, readymade for any other social environment they might encounter. And yet, this is exactly what the behaviorist myth of auto-individuation presupposes, an excellent example of the power of code applied to material bodies, as well as the abstract value placed on behaviorism as a set of social technologies.

Of course, this also contradicts basic principles of human development. To return to what was discussed above, it is essential for any child to remain sensitive to their unique predispositions to certain things, as well as their unique capacities for affect, in order to learn steadily more complex behaviors (i.e., language) over time. Any attempt to couple fear or a threat response with certain behaviors is inherently violent, insofar as it risks disconnecting a person's locus of motivation from their bodily ability to understand affect. This is true even if this behavior is interpreted as chaos (e.g., in the form of stimming) "from the outside." In the words of physicist Michael Baranger (2001), for instance, it is only on the "edge of chaos," and thus also the edge of risk—where the degrees of complexity involve not only an "interplay between cooperation and competition" but also "between chaos and non-chaos" (essentially an "interplay between scales")—that evolution can be elicited across otherwise discrete dynamical systems (p. 9). At this juncture, we find ourselves far removed from the "old cliche of 'the survival of the fittest', which has done so much damage to the understanding of evolution in the public's mind" (p. 10).

This dynamic becomes especially relevant, and exceedingly complex, in a world where children grow up with access to information technologies that allow them to connect to an entire ecosystem of others—a cornucopia of concepts, percepts, and relations—all without moving anything but their fingers. And yet, it is important to remember that how the material movements produced through a particular computer–human interface is interpreted by a group of researchers, or a clinician, is likely to differ notably from how those same movements are incorporated into the schemas of any bodies integrating such tools into their unique affective rhythms (see Parsons et al., 2019). Again, defining any set of individual behaviors primarily according to the risks they might pose to others, or even oneself, reinforces a logic of exclusion, which places arbitrary constraint on the technical platforms through which those with notable neurological variations might express themselves. It is often only at the edges of society, hence the edges of "noise," that such bodies, given their idiosyncratic forms of expression, can interact creatively with available technologies in ways that might otherwise be restricted from their onset.

From collective self-advocacy to network subjectivities

Hacking, as described above, is typically carried out to subvert the overarching rules of a system, not simply to create chaos but to disrupt the constraints already imposed on speech and technology-use (also considered a form of expression). This subversion is necessary precisely because of the highly regulated protocols of capitalism—the same ones underpinning the appropriation of "mental health" through apparatuses of control. Insofar as psychological theories and practices have become repurposed as social technologies to support control protocols, the social character of "the hacker" provides a useful lens for thinking about how psychology might be re-imaged under a different logic of collective power. Considering how the history of psy-disciplines are inextricable from the more general goals related to social engineering, it seems only appropriate to repurpose their tools in ways that can subvert these very goals.

This is precisely the move that many disability activist groups, including the neurodiversity movement,[3] have already been implementing for decades. As Kapp (2020) describes:

> The [neurodiversity] movement arguably adopts a spectrum or dimensional concept to neurodiversity, in which people's neurocognitive differences largely have no natural boundaries. While the extension from this concept to group-based identity politics that distinguish between the neurodivergent and neurotypical may at first seem contradictory, the neurodiversity framework draws from reactions to existing stigma- and mistreatment-inducing medical categories *imposed* on people that they *reclaim* by negotiating their meaning into an affirmative construct. (p. 2, emphasis in original)

Reclaiming terms like *Autistic*, *Aspie*, and even *neuro*-divergent are, as such, all examples of activists hacking the meaning of psy-concepts for regionally specific informational and affective needs. Dyck and Russell (2020) trace the roots of neurodiversity to "Mad pride, the disability rights movement, the recovery movement, and other consumer/survivor movements [that] emerged alongside these intellectual critiques of psychiatry" underpinning deinstitutionalization movements of the 1960s (p. 169). What all these movements have in common is a direct challenge to the exclusive authority granted to psychiatry as the dominant voice regarding the many different spectrums and expressions of non-normative experience.

On one hand, it is important to understand the legacy of a movement. It makes sense to connect the emergence of the neurodiversity movement to earlier consumer rights and anti-psychiatry movements, since they have common stakes and likely spring from common experiences of subjugation. However, the neurodiversity movement gained momentum not through peer-lead mentor groups, conferences, or even in-person disability activism; it formed almost entirely across social networks formed initially online. As Karen Buckle (2020) explains:

> Soon after I first discovered the Internet in late 1996, I sought out autism-related groups and immediately went to spending hours every day on autism chat rooms on Internet Relay Chat (IRC) and email-based support groups ("lists") such as Independent Living on the Autistic Spectrum... and Autism. Through these activities, I heard about Autreat and joined ANI-L, the list run by the organization responsible for Autreat, Autism Network International (ANI, www.autismnetworkinternational.org). (p. 109)

Stories like these are common in the neurodiversity movement and among other autistic activists. The ideas underpinning the neurodiversity paradigm began taking off in the early 2000s, through media shared on web forums like *Aspergia*, *AutAdvo*, *Aspies for Freedom*, *The Autist*, *Autcom*, *Angelfre*, *Wrongplanet* and *Neurodiversity.com* (Dyck & Russell, 2020). Many of such websites take an explicitly educational tone, spreading information and warning about disinformation regarding autism and associated conditions. According to Kathleen Seidel (2020), the mother of an autistic son, for instance:

> I continued to read and squirrel away URLs, increasingly gravitating to work by autistic authors. I delved into essays by Jim Sinclair, Frank Klein, Larry Arnold, and Joelle (then Joel) Smith. I discovered the writings of Michelle Dawson...Laura Tisoncik's and Mel (then Amanda) Baggs's "Institute for the Study of the Neurologically Typical"...made a strong impression, and both eventually became friends. Janet Norman-Bain's "Oops ...Wrong Planet! Syndrome" website led to hours of exploration. (p. 90)

Seidel, who would later go on to create the website *neurodiversity.com*, reports being irrevocably changed through this process. Given everything she learned, she began seeing autistic characteristics in her own mother, father, and even herself, noting "traits like intense focus; bluntness; anxiety and occasional sensory overload; fondness for collecting, organizing, and diving deeply into subjects that interest me" (p. 91). Neumeier and Brown (2020), both of whom are also autistic, describe a similarly circuitous route. It was through their shared concern about the JRC that they met, and both learned about abuses happening there separately through different blogs and websites operated by autistic activists.

Meg Evan's (2020) story is especially relevant to the links between autism, digital cultures, and the neurodiversity paradigm. Evans describes the experience of bouncing around from school to school as a child, never really knowing why, only to grow up to find out it was because they did not want her there. When first coming across information about autism online, it was mostly couched in a discourse of epidemic and mass hysteria, until she came across the website Aspergia. From there, Evans met a supportive group of fellow autistics, many of whom ended up starting their own websites. Shortly thereafter, Evans came across a webpage about new research on genetic screening for autism, which proposed that within ten years, genetic testing would allow for prenatal detection of autism. And yet, Evans explains that:

> What I found most unsettling about this statement was not simply the fact that it had been made, but that the worldview from which it sprang was devoid of meaningful examination. The overall tenor of the article—and, indeed, of the general public discourse surrounding autism at the time—was that everyone agreed the world should not have autistic people in it. The only question, as many saw it, was how to reach that goal. An entire layer of critical inquiry into the underlying assumptions had been effectively short-circuited. (p. 128)

From here, Evans went on to post an "Autistic Genocide Clock" on her fanfiction site Ventura33 to spread awareness about the dangers of such a perspective. The page got so many hits that it eventually had to moved to a virtual private server to keep up with the traffic.

Evans' story highlights how concerns about genetics and neurological development were at the center of both popular and clinical discourses on autism when the neurodiversity movement started gaining popularity. This was just after the conclusion of the human genome project, when scientists thought incorrectly that they were on the verge of unlocking the biological secrets to all human ailments. It is thus no surprise that these were the concerns through which the neurodiversity paradigm was initially shaped. Disavowing the medical lens of illness and cure, they nonetheless made considerable use of biology and technology in amplifying concerns shared with others like themselves. Unlike earlier movements, like anti-psychiatry and psychiatric survivors—both of whom are highly skeptical of biological explanations—neurodiversity activists borrow terms and concepts freely from such research programs, often applying them proudly as personal identifiers. The term autistic, for instance, is often described as a certain "phenotype" rather than a diagnosis in the DSM. The idea of *diversity* in neurodiversity is not, as such, simply some mundane appeal for greater inclusion across otherwise disparate and disconnected groups. It serves as a direct rebuke of what still is a very real existential threat to a future group of humans that, prior to the neurodiversity category, might not have had any other links in common. Timothy Morton (2017), for instance, repurposes the term *species* to describe such emergent collectives, which points in turn to Deligny's concept of species as the patterns produced by a body with its environment rather than some "code" hidden deep within it. While such a large number of genes have now been identified with autism that any such phenotype would likely prove impossible to detect with accuracy in utero, if the autism-vaccine "debate" is any indication, that will not stop people from trying.

Neumeier and Brown (2020) echo simlar desires as Evans for action in the face of injustice and collective trauma, with Neumeier described as harboring deeply seated animal welfare concerns and Brown mentioned as being highly critical of the way the events from 9/11 were appropriated to carry out attacks on people of color under the auspice of an ongoing "war on terror." The former two are also lawyers serving primarily structurally marginalized populations. On a theoretical level, such links make sense insofar as a relatively intense focus on particularities and being not easily swayed by popular opinion are both experiences commonly described by autistic people (Kapp & Ne'eman, 2020). *Becoming-autistic*, in these ways, thus represents a limit point for capitalism, where the protocols of control societies no longer modulate experience as intended but are instead repurposed by those who are able to *read* between the social gaps that others tend to overlook (see Skott-Myhre & Taylor, 2011). Here, pre-individual packets of trauma, and the individual identities associated with them, can be transformed into collective action through a shared concern for each other and the world in ways that exhibit, creatively, the very capacities of empathy and taking another's perspective that are often cited as what autistic people *lack*, as well as the reasons why they are often treated differently than everybody else (Leudar et al., 2004). This can thus be understood in terms of what John Roberts (2017) describes, for instance, as "taking up traumatic ethics," which:

> is to embrace a socio-historically situated solidarity with those beings who share our epochal mode of withdrawal...align ourselves with practices that touch the ontological structure of trauma...and question the exportation of technologies that would traumatize others in non-Western [or non-normative] contexts...as well it is to cease our own collusion with the 'fascism in us all, in our heads and our everyday behavior, the fascism that causes us to love power, to desire the very thing that dominates and exploits us' (Foucault, 1983, p. xiii). (p. 203)

Of course, the neurodiversity movement does not speak for all those who have experiences "outside the norm," or even all people on the autism-spectrum. It is also an unhelpful, and possibly harmful, stereotype to assume all autistic people like computers or prefer to use technology to communicate. However, when it comes to the neurodiversity movement, specifically, their unique modes of being in a network highlight certain capacities of digital technology that are often obscured by discourses related to "tech-hysteria," for instance, in analogous fashion to the way capacities of autistic people are obscured by discourses related to the "autism epidemic."

The network of neurodivergent cultures overviewed so far emerged to create a virtual ecosystem of social support and information flow for individuals who had been targeted by others throughout much of their lives, largely for acting in ways deemed "outside the norm." Many of them did not have the language available to describe their experiences—they simply felt like outcasts. Through fortuitous connections and new narratives found online, however, they wove highly supportive social networks that allowed many without a voice to develop one, often by starting with a keyboard instead of their mouth. Whether this includes digital technology, as such, it almost certainly is the case that any *body* occupying a place at the edge of society will have its own idiosyncratic mechanisms for stimulating affective capacities creatively, and it will undoubtedly benefit from sharing space with others who embody similar pre-individual investments fields and predispositions. Henderson et al. (2014), for instance, describe this mode of expression in terms of "cyborg writing, admixing constraints and opportunities in a way that opens alternative, polycentric, and indeterminate but nonetheless important political possibilities for people on (and off) the AS" (p. 504). By repurposing scientific vernacular from studies found online, and tracing publicly the limits of scientific knowledge while not renouncing it completely, early neurodiversity activists had effectively begun a process of "hacking the master code of [their] ontological and epistemological inheritance in ways that both define and disrupt the boundaries of autism and the way in which [they] explain the world to each other and to [themselves]" (p. 520).

Drawing on Simondon, again, we can understand such cyborg expressions as constituting collective networks of transindividuation, a possible extension of Guattari's concept of collective assemblages of enunciation, over and against the psychological myths of auto-individuation outlined above. This likewise returns us to the two qualities distinguishing Simondon's theory of information from general cybernetics: interoperability and indeterminacy. Interoperability, referring to the convergence of several different streams of information in ways that effectively contribute to multiple orders of information, and indeterminacy, to how information is never stable, or its transmission fully complete, largely because of the ways pre-individual fields merge into nascent transindividual threads, which are modulated uniquely from one social situation to the next.

The paradigm constructed through the neurodiversity movement, for instance, could not have emerged within any other social network—like the hearing voices network (HVN) (Hearing Voices Network, 2020), for instance. Members of HVN have their own predispositions and affective capacities corresponding with their unique natures and technologies at their disposal. According to its website, HVN is composed are largely of "people who hear voices, see visions, or have other unusual perceptions" that mental health professionals have long described as symptoms of schizophrenia. In contrast with the neurodiversity movement, moreover, HVN is organized largely through trainings, conferences, and workshops conducted in-person and usually on a local scale. And yet, HVN and the neurodiversity movement share in common an expressed fidelity to the inherent value of non-normative experiences, and a commitment to amplifying any mechanism that guards these experiences from being captured by the paranoiac machines of capitalism.

Walker's (2014) distinction between the neurodiversity paradigm and neurodiversity movement is important here, as well, considering the possibility for the paradigm to become concretized in a way whereby it is transformed into an object of collective desire for interests beyond the movement itself. Groups composed of mental health professionals and parents, for instance, tend to act on behalf of their own pre-individual investments and social values. At the same time, no social movement lasts forever, and it is common for ideas from a movement to become appropriated as they become concretized into a paradigm. With reference to the corporatization of the term "neurodiversity" above, its cooption by mainstream institutions might have already begun. The future of the neurodiversity movement can certainly still go in any number of yet realized directions, and yet, as with any collective, it is up to its constituents to diagnose their collective symptoms as signs of problems most relevant to their own lives.

This is precisely why Deleuze (1990), drawing on Spinoza, understands affections of the body as public signs of events that have already occurred, of which the mind typically lags behind in its interpretations. The general meaning of *syndrome*, as a collection of signs correlated with one another, is relevant here, as signs do not create their own meanings; they can only be conferred meaning based on culturally relative and historically conditioned problems, which are in turn identified by those granted authority in a respective field of knowledge. When it comes to fields like psychiatry and psychology, there is no shortage of historical examples where syndromes and symptoms have been defined by professionals without any reference to the problems most relevant to those diagnosed. Moving forward, it remains to be seen which symptom-signs will coalesce into which identified syndromes, and likewise which social groups' interests will be served most by the contours of such constellations.

Groups like the neurodiversity movement, on the other hand, have taken it upon themselves to in-form the world about their self-identified problems, inventing new capacities for thought, affect, and action in the process. It is certainly no coincidence that online message boards and websites have served as vital tools throughout the movement as they were both just becoming available and perfectly suited for the informational needs of activists at the time. Beyond the neurodiversity movement's use of the internet however, it no longer makes sense to talk about "mental health" without reference to the digital multimedia landscapes in which most contemporary social relationships are embedded. Online social networks operate in ways that allow a single person to assume multiple identities under different avatars or accounts, in turn affording the user multiple avenues to receive information about one or several topics simultaneously. In an "offline" world in which behaviors are either reinforced or punished through direct contact with others, there are certain meta-cognitive (i.e., second-order) constraints placed on expression. With online platforms, by contrast, any given user can embody a range of communication patterns and thus experiment interactively without fear of immediate retribution. Positions that can be taken up in conversation are essentially as variable as the user can imagine and is willing to perform, offering multiple channels for expressing affect with platforms that transcend any one individual. This manner of using technologies for highly collective purposes is, as such, an inherently (ethico)aesthetic process that does not presuppose the existence of any single notion of the individual despite being sustained through singular expressions of subjectivation (Guattari, 1995).

In their book, *Anti-Oedipus*, Delueze and Guattari (2009) suggest that:

> [d]esire does not *lack* anything… [i]t is, rather, the *subject* that is missing in desire, or desire that lacks a fixed subject; there is no fixed subject unless there is repression. Desire and its object are one and the same thing: the machine, as a machine of a machine. Desire is a machine, and the object of desire is another machine connected to it. Hence, the product is something removed or deducted from the process of producing. (p. 26)

Here, desire is understood as an immanent surplus of kinetic activity rather than a psychological deficiency—a mode of machinic production that cannot be fixed permanently to an ideal standard, like "an individual," precisely because bodies and technologies are both open systems that feed information indeterminately into each other. Their respective habits and recursive loops are alternately modulated and broken down through the links they form with each other, engendering temporary platforms whereby pre-individual fields can mutate into what Deleuze and Guattari (2009) describe as *desiring-machines*. No machine operates on its own. By becoming "interoperable" with technologies that are appropriately calibrated for their amplification, singular capacities for action and desire can yield new modes of sociotechnical expression that did not exist before. And in these ways, technologies, pre-individual fields, and other relevant cultural factors can be incorporated into collective networks of transindividuation, with each element becoming refashioned in the formation of affect and technical expression rather than serving merely as "an individual" within some artificial or strictly digitized system.

Given that individuals in collective self-advocacy networks like the neurodiversity movement, hearing voices, and other mad pride groups occupy the place of objects for psy-disciplines, they are uniquely positioned to deconstruct contemporary "mental health" technologies and repurpose any useful parts for their respective social purposes. Rather than operating automatically as mechanisms within broader myths of auto-individuation, such machinic processes produce value immanently and relationally in the ongoing experimentation with sensation and thought. And yet, given the ways digital technology is employed so widely for surveillance and behavioral control, it is imperative that such processes extend to the data collected about such group, as well, which, given the right set of technologies, can likewise be repurposed to build stronger communities outside of any and all reference to "mental health" (e.g., Kostakis & Bauwens, 2014). While social identities can play a useful role in this process—providing, for instance, mediums of expression—they cannot simply be substituted for the desires and affective investments that have kept these movements alive so far. Such acts of misidentification, to the contrary, simply open the door for protocols of control underlying contemporary capitalist markets to more easily disarm these movements, by appropriating the technologies they have created and turning them into mechanisms that capture the desire otherwise expressed with those very tools.

Notes

1 Deligny described this as a form of "primodial communism," not as a system of governance but as a way of organizing life together based on overlaps across space, desire, and need. This bears similarities with Timothy Morton's (2017) reconceptualization of communism beyond the quasi-humanism of Marx, into a form of solidarity with nonhuman people.
2 This is the same organizational logic Hannah Arendt (1998) points to, for instance, when noting that:

> The trouble with modern theories of behaviorism is not that they are wrong but that they could become true, that they actually are the best possible conceptualization of certain obvious trends in modern society. It is quite conceivable that the modern age–which began with such an unprecedented and promising outburst of human activity–may end in the deadliest, most sterile passivity history has ever known. (p. 322)

3 It is important to note that not all individuals who have received or meet the criteria for a diagnosis of ASD agree with the tenets of the neurodiversity paradigm, and the movement has received criticism from those both on and off the spectrum. For a list of some of the more popular criticisms, as well as possible rebukes, see Russell (2020). For the purposes of this book, Walker's (2014) distinction between the neurodiversity movement and the neurodiversity paradigm is maintained to highlight how they have both taken on different meanings as the term neurodiversity has become more widely circulated.

REFERENCES

Abraham, T. H. (2002). (Physio)logical circuits: The intellectual origins of the McCulloch–Pitts neural networks. *Journal of the History of the Behavioral Sciences*, *38*(1), 3–25. doi:10.1002/jhbs.1094.

Allen, D. (2009). From boundary concept to boundary object: The practice and politics of care pathway development. *Social Science & Medicine*, *69*, 354–361. doi:10.1016/j.socscimed.2009.05.002.

American Psychiatric Association, American Psychiatric Association, & DSM-5 Task Force. (2013). *Diagnostic and Statistical Manual of Mental Disorders: DSM-5*. Washington, D.C.: American Psychiatric Association.

Arendt, H. (1998). *The Human Condition*. Chicago, IL: University of Chicago Press.

Barad, K. (2007). *Meeting the Universe Halfway: Quantum Physics and the Entanglement of Matter and Meaning* (Second Printing edition). Durham: Duke University Press Books.

Baranger, M. (2001). *Chaos, complexity, and entropy: A physics talk for non-physicists*. New England Complex Systems Institute. Retrieved from https://www.researchgate.net/publication/235361203_Chaos_Complexity_and_Entropy_A_physics_talk_for_non-physicists

Barbash, E. (2017, January 25). Reasons to not use insurance for mental health treatment. *Tampa Therapy*. Retrieved from https://tampatherapy.com/2017/01/25/reasons-not-use-insurance-mental-health-treatment/

Baron-Cohen, S. (2008). *Autism and Asperger Syndrome* (1st edition). Oxford: Oxford University Press.

Bateson, G. (1971). The cybernetics of "self": A theory of alcoholism. *Psychiatry: Journal for the Study of Interpersonal Processes*, *34*, 1–18.

Bateson, G. (1987). *Steps to an Ecology of Mind: Collected Essays in Anthropology, Psychiatry, Evolution, and Epistemology*. Chicago: Jason Aronson Inc.

Bateson, G., Jackson, D. D., Haley, J., & Weakland, J. (1956). Toward a theory of schizophrenia. *Behavioral Science, 1*(4), 251–264. doi:10.1002/bs.3830010402.

Beach, S., Foran, H., Heyman, R., Smith, A., Cordaro, A., Wamboldt, M., & Kaslow, N. (2016). Relational processes: Historical background, current considerations, and future directions for DSM-5 and ICD-11. In K. T. Sullivan & E. Lawrence (Eds.), *The Oxford Handbook of Relationship Science and Couple Interventions* (pp. 7–18). Oxford: Oxford University Press.

Bearman, S. K., Wadkins, M., Bailin, A., & Doctoroff, G. (2015). Pre-practicum training in professional psychology to close the research–practice gap: Changing attitudes toward evidence-based practice. *Training and Education in Professional Psychology, 9*(1), 13–20. https://doi.org/10.1037/tep0000052

Beck, T. J. (2020). From cybernetic networks to social narratives: Mapping value in mental health systems beyond individual psychopathology. *Journal of Theoretical and Philosophical Psychology, 40*(2), 85–106. https://doi.org/10.1037/teo0000127

Beck, T., & Friedman, E. (2019, February). *What can network theory say about pathology in the internet age?* National paper presentation at American Psychology Association, Division 24 mid-winter conference, Nashville, TN.

Beck, U. (1992). *Risk Society: Towards a New Modernity* (1st edition). London: SAGE Publications Ltd.

Blume, H. (1998, September). Neurodiversity: On the neurological underpinnings of geekdom. *The Atlantic*. Retrieved from www.theatlantic.com/magazine/archive/1998/09/neurodiversity/305909.

Bly, N. (2012). *Ten Days in a Mad-House* (Null edition). Rockville, MD: A Nellie Bly Book.

Boden, M. (2008). *Mind as Machine: A History of Cognitive Science.* Oxford and New York: Oxford University Press.

Bourdieu, P. (1986). The forms of capital. In J. G. Richardson (Ed.), *Handbook of Theory and Research for the Sociology of Education* (pp. 241–58). New York: Greenwood Press.

Borsboom, D. (2017). A network theory of mental disorders. *World Psychiatry, 16*, 5–13. doi:10.1002/wps.20375.

Bradley, E. (1984, December). *MK-ULTRA/MIND CONTROL EXPERIMENTS | CIA FOIA (foia.cia.gov).* Retrieved from www.cia.gov/library/readingroom/document/cia-rdp91-00901r000500150005-5.

Buckle, K. L. (2020). Autscape. In S. K. Kapp (Ed.), *Autistic Community and the Neurodiversity Movement: Stories from the Frontline* (pp. 109–122). Singapore: Palgrave Macmillan. doi:10.1007/978-981-13-8437-0_8.

Canguilhem, G. (1989). *The Normal and the Pathological.* New York: Zone Books.

Carveth, D. L. (1984). The analyst's metaphors: A deconstructionist perspective. *Psychoanalysis & Contemporary Thought, 7*(4), 491–560.

Chalmers, D. J. (1997). *The Conscious Mind: In Search of a Fundamental Theory* (Revised edition). New York: Oxford University Press.

Chaney, A. (2017). *Runaway: Gregory Bateson, the Double Bind, and the Rise of Ecological Consciousness.* Chapel Hill: The University of North Carolina Press.

References

Châtelet, G. (2014). *To Live and Think Like Pigs: The Incitement of Envy and Boredom in Market Democracies* (Robin Mackay, Trans.). New York: Urbanomic and Sequence Press.

Chitsabesan P., & Hughes N. (2016). Mental health needs and neurodevelopmental disorders amongst young offenders: Implications for policy and practice. In J. Winstone (Ed.), *Mental Health, Crime and Criminal Justice*. London: Palgrave Macmillan.

Christiaens, T. (2016). Digital subjectivation and financial markets: Criticizing Social Studies of Finance with Lazzarato. *Big Data & Society, 3*(2), 2053951716662897. https://doi.org/10.1177/2053951716662897

Chomsky, N. (1967). A review of B. F. Skinner's verbal behavior. In L. A. Jakobovits & M. S. Miron (Eds.), *Readings in the Psychology of Language* (pp. 142–143). New York: Prentice-Hall.

Clarke, B. (2014). *Neocybernetics and Narrative*. Minnesota Press. Retrieved from www.upress.umn.edu/book-division/books/neocybernetics-and-narrative.

Cohen, J. D., Noll, D. C., & Schneider W. (1993). Functional magnetic resonance imaging: Overview and methods for psychological research. *Behavioral Research Methods Instrumental Computing, 25*, 101–113.

Coleman, E. G. (2012). *Coding Freedom: The Ethics and Aesthetics of Hacking*. Princeton, NJ: Princeton University Press.

Coleman, G. (2011). Hacker politics and publics. *Public Culture, 23*, 3(65), 511–516. doi:10.1215/08992363-1336390.

Collins, S. G. (2007). *Do cyborgs dream of electronic rats? The Macy conferences and the emergence of hybrid multi-agent systems*, 25–33.

Connolly, M. (2008). The remarkable logic of autism: Developing and describing an embedded curriculum based in semiotic phenomenology. *Sport, Ethics and Philosophy, 2*(2), 234–256.

Cordeschi, R. (1991). The discovery of the artificial. Some protocybernetic developments 1930–1940. *AI & Society, 5*(3), 218–238. doi:10.1007/BF01891917.

Cordeschi, R. (2002). Cybernetics and the origins of artificial intelligence. In R. Cordeschi (Ed.), *The Discovery of the Artificial: Behavior, Mind and Machines Before and Beyond Cybernetics* (pp. 153–186). Netherlands: Springer. https://doi.org/10.1007/978-94-015-9870-5_5

Cosgrove, L., & Karter, J. M. (2018). The poison in the cure: Neoliberalism and contemporary movements in mental health. *Theory & Psychology, 28*(5), 669–683. doi:10.1177/0959354318796307.

Cosgrove, L., & Krimsky, S. (2012). A comparison of DSM-IV and DSM-5 panel members' financial associations with industry: A pernicious problem persists. *PLOS Medicine, 9*(3), e1001190. doi:10.1371/journal.pmed.1001190.

Curran, T., & Hill, A. P. (2017). Perfectionism is increasing over time: A meta-analysis of birth cohort differences from 1989 to 2016. *Psychological Bulletin.* Advance online publication. doi:10.1037/bul0000138.

Cuthbert, B. N., & Insel, T. R. (2013). Toward the future of psychiatric diagnosis: The seven pillars of RDoC. *BMC Medicine, 11*, 126. doi:10.1186/1741-7015-11-126.

Damasio, A. (2005). *Descartes' Error: Emotion, Reason, and the Human Brain* (Reprint edition). London: Penguin Books.

Davar, B. (2014). Globalizing psychiatry and the case of 'vanishing' alternatives in a neo-colonial state. *Disability and the Global South, 1,* 266–284.

Dawson, M. (2004). *The Misbehaviour of Behaviourists. No Autistics Allowed.* Retrieved January 12, 2020, from www.sentex.ca/~nexus23/naa_aba.html.

Deacon, B. J. (2013). The biomedical model of mental disorder: A critical analysis of its validity, utility, and effects on psychotherapy research. *Clinical Psychology Review, 33*(7), 846–861. doi:10.1016/j.cpr.2012.09.007.

Deleuze, G. (1990). *The Logic of Sense* (C. V. Boundas, Ed.; M. Lester & C. Stivale, Trans.; Reprint edition). New York: Columbia University Press.

Deleuze, G. (1992). Postscript on the Societies of Control, October, vol. 59, pp. 3–7.

Deleuze, G. (2004). *Desert Islands and Other Texts, 1953–1974* (Mike Taormina, Trans.). New York: Semiotext(e).

Deleuze, G. (2007). On Spinoza: Lectures by Gilles Deleuze. Retrieved from http://deleuzelectures.blogspot.com/2007/02/on-spinoza.html.

Deleuze, G., & Guattari, F. (1987). *A Thousand Plateaus: Capitalism and Schizophrenia* (B. Massumi, Trans.; 1st edition). Minneapolis: University of Minnesota Press.

Deleuze, G., & Guattari, F. (2009). *Anti-Oedipus: Capitalism and Schizophrenia* (R. Hurley, Ed.; M. Seem & H. Lane, Trans.; 6th printing). New York: Penguin Classics.

Deligny, F. (2015). *The Arachnean and Other Texts* (D. S. Burk & C. Porter, Trans.; 1st edition). Minneapolis, MN: Univocal Publishing.

Deyoung, C., & Krueger, R. F. (2018). Understanding psychopathology: Cybernetics and psychology on the boundary between order and chaos. *Psychological Inquiry, 29,* 165–174. doi:10.1080/1047840X.2018.1513690.

Dhar, A. (2019). *Madness and Subjectivity* (1st edition). London and New York: Routledge.

Donders, F. C. (1869). On the speed of mental processes: Attention and Performance II. *Acta Psychologica, 30,* 412–431.

Dumit, J. (2004). *Picturing Personhood: Brain images and Biomedical Identity.* Princeton, NJ: Princeton University Press.

Dyck, E., & Russell, G. (2020). Challenging psychiatric classification: Healthy autistic diversity and the neurodiversity movement. In S. J. Taylor & A. Brumby (Eds.), *Healthy Minds in the Twentieth Century: In and Beyond the Asylum* (pp. 167–187). Cham: Springer. doi:10.1007/978-3-030-27275-3_8.

Edwards, Paul. (2000). Machine in the middle: Cybernetic psychology and WWII. In R. Chrisley & S. Begeer (Eds.), *Artificial Intelligence: Critical Concepts* (pp. 338–370). London and New York: Taylor & Francis.

Ekbia, H. R., & Nardi, B. A. (2017). *Heteromation, and Other Stories of Computing and Capitalism.* Cambridge, MA: The MIT Press.

Eng, M. (2015). Deterritorialising transversality: The antagonism of the object between Deleuze and Guattari. *Parallax, 21*(4), 448–461. doi:10.1080/13534645.2015.1086530.

References

Evans, M. (2020). The autistic genocide clock. In S. K. Kapp (Ed.), *Autistic Community and the Neurodiversity Movement: Stories from the Frontline* (pp. 123–132). Singapore: Springer. doi:10.1007/978-981-13-8437-0_9.

Fanon, F. (2008). *Black Skin, White Masks* (R. Philcox, Trans.; Revised edition). New York: Grove Press.

Ferrando, F. (2014). Posthumanism, transhumanism, antihumanism, metahumanism, and new materialisms: Differences and relations. *Existenz, 8*, 26–32.

Feest, U. (2012). Exploratory experiments, concept formation, and theory construction in psychology. In U. Feest & F. Steinle (Eds.), *Scientific Concepts and Investigative Practice* (pp. 3–167). Berlin: De Gruyter.

Fibiger, H. C. (2012). Psychiatry, the pharmaceutical industry, and the road to better therapeutics. *Schizophrenia Bulletin, 38*, 649–650.

Floridi, L. (2014). *The Fourth Revolution: How the Infosphere is Reshaping Human Reality* (Reprint edition). Oxford: Oxford University Press.

Foucault, M. (1983). The subject and power." In H. Dreyfus & P. Rabinow (Eds.), *Beyond Structuralism and Hermeneutics* (pp. 208–226). Chicago: The University of Chicago Press.

Foucault, M. (2003). *"Society Must Be Defended": Lectures at the Collège de France, 1975–1976* (D. Macey, Trans.; Reprint edition). New York: Picador.

Foucault, M. (2008). *Psychiatric Power: Lectures at the Collège de France, 1973–1974* (J. Lagrange, G. Burchell, & A. I. Davidson, Eds.). New York: Picador.

Freud, S. (1915). The unconscious. In J. Strachey et al. (Trans.), *The Standard Edition of the Complete Psychological Works of Sigmund Freud* (Vol. XIX). London: Hogarth Press.

Freud, S. (1921). *Group Psychology and the Analysis of the Ego* (Vol. XVIII, pp. 65–144). London: Hogarth Press.

Freud, S. (1922). *Beyond the Pleasure Principle* (C. J. M. Hubback, Trans.). London and Vienna: International Psycho-Analytical.

Freud, S. (1923). The ego and the Id. In J. Strachey et al. (Trans.), *The Standard Edition of the Complete Psychological Works of Sigmund Freud* (Vol. XIX). London: Hogarth Press.

Freud, S. (1925 [1924]). Notiz über den "Wunderblok." *Internationale Zeitschrift für Psychoanalyse, 11*, 1–5; A note upon the mystic writing pad. SE, 19: 227–232.

Freud, S. (1933). XXXIIe des Nouvelles Conférences, « Angoisse et vie pulsionnelle », GW XV; SE, XXII.

Garland, D. (2003). "The Rise of Risk," In R. V. Ericson & A. Doyle (Eds.), *Risk and Morality* (Green College Thematic Lecture Series). Toronto: University of Toronto Press.

Gaebel, W., Zielasek, J., & Reed, G. (2017). Mental and behavioural disorders in the ICD-11: Concepts, methodologies, and current status. *Psychiatria Polska, 51*(2), 169–175. doi:10.12740/PP/69660.

Galloway, A. (2001). Protocol, or, how control exists after decentralization. *Rethinking Marxism, 13*(3–4), 81–88. doi:10.1080/089356901101241758.

Galloway, A. R. (2004). *Protocol: How Control Exists after Decentralization*. Cambridge, MA: MIT Press.

Giddens, A. (1999). Risk and responsibility. *The Modern Law Review, 62*(1), 1–10. https://doi.org/10.1111/1468-2230.00188

Gomory, T., Wong, S. E., Cohen, D., & Lacasse, J. R. (2011). Clinical social work and the biomedical industrial complex. *Journal of Sociology and Social Welfare*. Retrieved from http://heinonlinebackup.com/hol-cgi-bin/get_pdf.cgi?handle=hein.journals/jrlsasw38&section=43

Gray, N. S., Laing, J. M., & Noaks, L. (2013). *Criminal Justice, Mental Health and the Politics of Risk*. New York: Routledge.

Guattari, F. (1995). *Chaosmosis: An Ethico-aesthetic Paradigm*. Bloomington: Indiana University Press.

Guattari, F. (1996). In G. Genosko (Ed.), *The Guattari Reader* (1st edition). John Wiley & Sons.

Guattari, F. (2015). *Psychoanalysis and Transversality: Texts and Interviews 1955–1971* (A. Hodges, Trans.). South Pasadena, CA: Semiotext.

Guttman, N. (1977). On Skinner and Hull: A reminiscence and projection. *American Psychologist, 32*(5), 321–328. doi:10.1037/0003-066X.32.5.321.

Hacking, I. (2000). *The Social Construction of What?* Cambridge, MA: Harvard University Press.

Hacking, I. (2009). Humans, aliens & autism. *Daedalus, 138*(3), 44–59. https://doi.org/10.1162/daed.2009.138.3.44

Halpern, O. (2014). Cybernetic rationality. *Distinktion: Journal of Social Theory, 15*(2), 223–238. doi:10.1080/1600910X.2014.923320.

Halpern, O. (2015). *Beautiful Data: A History of Vision and Reason Since 1945*. Durham: Duke University Press.

Haraway, D. (1990). *Simians, Cyborgs, and Women: The Reinvention of Nature* (1st edition). New York: Routledge.

Haraway, D. (1996). Situated knowledges: The science question in feminism and privileged partial perspectives. In Keller, E. F., & Longino, H. E. (Eds.). *Feminism and Science* (Revised edition) (pp. 249–263). Oxford and New York: Oxford University Press.

Haraway, D. (2000). A cyborg manifesto science, technology, and socialist feminism in the late twentieth century. In B. M. Kennedy & D. Bell (Eds.), *The Cybercultures Reader* (1st edition). New York: Routledge.

Harries-Jones, P. (2008). Gregory Bateson's "Uncovery" of ecological aesthetics. In J. Hoffmeyer (Ed.), *A Legacy for Living Systems: Gregory Bateson as Precursor to Biosemiotics* (pp. 153–167). Springer Netherlands. doi:10.1007/978-1-4020-6706-8_11.

Hayles, N. K. (1999). *How We Became Posthuman: Virtual Bodies in Cybernetics, Literature, and Informatics* (1st edition). Chicago, IL: University Of Chicago Press.

Hayles, N. K. (2001). Desiring agency: Limiting metaphors and enabling constraints in Dawkins and Deleuze/Guattari. *Substance, 30*(1), 144–159.

Hearing Voices Network. (2020). *Hearing Voices Network: About HVN*. Retrieved from www.hearing-voices.org/about-us/.

Heidbreder, E. (1939). *Seven Psychologies*. New York: D. Appleton-Century.

Heims, S. J. (1991). *The Cybernetics Group*. Cambridge, MA: MIT Press.

Henderson, V., Davidson, J., Hemsworth, K., & Edwards, S. (2014). Hacking the master code: Cyborg stories and the boundaries of autism. *Social & Cultural Geography*, 15(5), 504–524. doi:10.1080/14649365.2014.898781.

Hengartner, M. P., Jakobsen, J. C., Sørensen, A., & Plöderl, M. (2019, November 12). Efficacy of new-generation antidepressants assessed with the Montgomery-Asberg depression rating scale, the gold standard clinician rating scale: A meta-analysis of randomized placebo-controlled trials. doi:10.31219/osf.io/3tuzy.

Hilton, L. (2015). *Mapping the Wander Lines: The Quiet Revelations of Fernand Deligny*. Retrieved from https://lareviewofbooks.org/article/mapping-the-wander-lines-the-quiet-revelations-of-fernand-deligny/

Huckvale, K., Torous, J., & Larsen, M. E. (2019). Assessment of the Data Sharing and Privacy Practices of Smartphone Apps for Depression and Smoking Cessation. *JAMA Network Open*, 2(4), e192542–e192542. doi:10.1001/jamanetworkopen.2019.2542.

Hui, Y. (2015). Modulation after control. *New Formations*, 84–85, 74.

Hull, C. L. (1943). *Principles of Behavior*. New York: D. Appleton-Century.

Hull, C. L., & Baernstein, H. D. (1929). A mechanical parallel to the conditioned reflex. *Science*, 70(1801), 14–15. doi:10.1126/science.70.1801.14-a.

Hutchins, E. (2010). Cognitive ecology. *Topics in Cognitive Science*, 2(4), 705–715.

Iliadis, A. (2013). Informational ontology: The meaning of Gilbert Simondon's concept of individuation. *Communication 1*, 2(1), 1–19. doi:10.7275/R59884XW.

Insel, T. R. (2007). Neuroscience: Shining light on depression. *Science*, 317, 757–758.

Insel, T. R. (2011). Mental illness defined as disruption in neural circuits. Retrieved February 18, 2012, from www.nimh.nih.gov/about/.

Insel, T. R. (2012). *NIMH » The Future of Psychiatry (= Clinical Neuroscience)*. Retrieved January 8, 2020, from www.nimh.nih.gov/about/directors/thomas-insel/blog/2012/the-future-of-psychiatry-clinical-neuroscience.shtml.

Jablonka, E., & Lamb, M. J. (2005). *Evolution in Four Dimensions: Genetic, Epigenetic, Behavioral, and Symbolic Variation in the History of Life* (1st edition). Cambridge, MA: A Bradford Book.

Jackson, G. B. (2010). *Contemporary Viewpoints on Human Intellect and Learning*. New York: Xlibris Corporation.

Johnstone, L. & Boyle, M. with Cromby, J., Dillon, J., Harper, D., Kinderman, P., Longden, E., Pilgrim, D. & Read, J. (2018). *The Power Threat Meaning Framework: Towards the Identification of Patterns in Emotional Distress, Unusual Experiences and Troubled or Troubling Behaviour, as an Alternative to Functional Psychiatric Diagnosis*. Leicester: British Psychological Society.

Jones, P. J., Heeren, A., & McNally, R. J. (2017). Commentary: A network theory of mental disorders. *Frontiers in Psychology*, 8. doi:10.3389/fpsyg.2017.01305.

Julesz, B. (1971). *Foundations of Cyclopean Perception*. Chicago, IL: University of Chicago Press.

Justman, S. (1994). Freud and his nephew. *Social Research*, 61, 457–476.

Kapp, S. K. (2020). Introduction. In S. K. Kapp (Ed.), *Autistic Community and the Neurodiversity Movement: Stories from the Frontline* (pp. 1–19). Singapore: Springer. doi:10.1007/978-981-13-8437-0_1.

Kapp, S. K., & Ne'eman, A. (2020). Lobbying autism's diagnostic revision in the DSM-5. In S. K. Kapp (Ed.), *Autistic Community and the Neurodiversity Movement: Stories from the Frontline* (pp. 167–194). Singapore: Springer. doi:10.1007/978-981-13-8437-0_13.

Kapp, S. K., Gillespie-Lynch, K., Sherman, L. E., & Hutman, T. (2013). Deficit, difference, or both? Autism and neurodiversity. *Developmental Psychology, 49*(1), 59–71. https://doi.org/10.1037/a0028353

Karter, J. M., & Kamens, S. R. (2019). Toward conceptual competence in psychiatric diagnosis: An ecological model for critiques of the DSM. In S. Steingard (Ed.), *Critical Psychiatry* (pp. 17–69). Cham: Springer. doi:10.1007/978-3-030-02732-2_2.

Keller, E. F., & Longino, H. E. (1996). Introduction. In Keller, E. F., & Longino, H. E. (Eds.), *Feminism and Science* (Revised edition) (pp. 1–16). Oxford and New York: Oxford University Press.

Kirmayer, L. J., & Pedersen, D. (2014). Toward a new architecture for global mental health. *Transcultural Psychiatry, 51*(6), 759–776. doi:10.1177/1363461514557202.

Klein, N. (2008). *The Shock Doctrine: The Rise of Disaster Capitalism* (1st edition). New York: Picador.

Klerman, G., Vaillant, G., Spitzer, R., & Michels, R. (1984). A debate on DSM-III: The advantages of DSM-III. *The American Journal of Psychiatry, 141*, 539–553.

Klin, A., Lin, D. J., Gorrindo, P., Ramsay, G., & Jones, W. (2009). Two-year-olds with autism orient to non-social contingencies rather than biological motion. *Nature, 459*(7244), 257–261. doi:10.1038/nature07868.

Kline, R. R. (2015). *The Cybernetics Moment: Or Why We Call Our Age the Information Age* (1st edition). Baltimore, MD: Johns Hopkins University Press.

Kostakis, V., & Bauwens, M. (2014). *Network Society and Future Scenarios for a Collaborative Economy*. Palgrave Macmillan. Retrieved from www.palgrave.com/us/book/9781137415066.

Kostka, G. (2019). China's social credit systems and public opinion: Explaining high levels of approval. *New Media & Society, 21*(7), 1565–1593. doi:10.1177/1461444819826402.

Kukreja, S., Kalra, G., Shah, N., & Shrivastava, A. (2013). Polypharmacy in psychiatry: A review. *Mens Sana Monographs, 11*(1), 82–99. doi:10.4103/0973-1229.104497.

Lacan, J. (1967) The Psychoanalytic Act, Book XV, The Seminar of Jacques Lacan.

Lacasse, J. R. (2014). After DSM-5 a critical mental health research agenda for the 21st century. *Research on Social Work Practice, 24*(1), 5–10. https://doi.org/10.1177/1049731513510048

Lacasse, J. R., & Gomory, T. (2003). Is graduate social work education promoting a critical approach to mental health practice? *Journal of Social Work Education, 39*(3), 383–408.

References

Leary, D. E. (Ed.). (1994). *Metaphors in the History of Psychology*. Cambridge, MA: Cambridge University Press.

Leonelli, S. (2016). *Data-Centric Biology: A Philosophical Study*. Chicago, IL: University of Chicago Press.

Leudar, I., & Costall, A. (2004). On the persistence of the 'problem of other minds' in psychology Chomsky, Grice and theory of mind. *Theory & Psychology, 14*(5), 601–621. doi:10.1177/0959354304046175.

Leudar, I., Costall, A., & Francis, D. (2004). Theory of mind: A critical assessment. *Theory & Psychology, 14*(5), 571–578. doi:10.1177/0959354304046173.

Luhmann, N. (2005). *Risk: A Sociological Theory* (1st Paperback edition). New Brunswick, NJ: Aldine Transaction.

Luxton, D. D. (Ed.). (2015). *Artificial Intelligence in Behavioral and Mental Health Care* (1st edition). Amsterdam and Boston: Academic Press.

MacDonald, R., Parry-Cruwys, D., Dupere, S., & Ahearn, W. (2014). Assessing progress and outcome of early intensive behavioral intervention for toddlers with autism. *Research in Developmental Disabilities, 35*(12), 3632–3644.

Malabou, C. (2012). *The New Wounded: From Neurosis to Brain Damage* (S. Miller, Trans.; 1st edition). New York: Fordham University Press.

Mayer-Schönberger, V., & Ramge, T. (2018). *Reinventing Capitalism in the Age of Big Data*. New York: Basic Books.

Mayes, R., & Horwitz, A. V. (2005). DSM-III and the revolution in the classification of mental illness. *Journal of the History of the Behavioral Sciences, 41*(3), 249–267.

McCulloch, W. S. (1954). McCulloch Papers, "*Physiology of Thinking and Perception,*" June 22. B: M139, Series III: Creative engineering, p. 1. Philadelphia, PA: American Philosophical Society.

McCulloch, W. S., & Pitts, W. (1943). A logical calculus of the ideas immanent in nervous activity. *The Bulletin of Mathematical Biophysics, 5*(4), 115–133. doi:10.1007/BF02478259.

McGrath, S. J. (2011). *The Dark Ground of Spirit* (1st edition). New York: Routledge.

McGuire, A. (2017). De-regulating disorder: On the rise of the spectrum as a neoliberal metric of human value. *Journal of Literary and Cultural Disability Studies, 11*, 403–421. doi:10.3828/jlcds.2017.32.

McNally, R. J. (2016). Can network analysis transform psychopathology? *Behaviour Research and Therapy, 86*, 95–104. doi:10.1016/j.brat.2016.06.006.

McNally, R. J., Robinaugh, D. J., Wu, G. W. Y., Wang, L., Deserno, M. K., & Borsboom, D. (2015). Mental disorders as causal systems a network approach to posttraumatic stress disorder. *Clinical Psychological Science, 3*(6), 836–849. doi:10.1177/2167702614553230.

Miller, G. A. (2003). The cognitive revolution: A historical perspective. *Trends in Cognitive Sciences, 7*(3), 141–144. doi:10.1016/S1364-6613(03)00029-9.

Mills, C. (2014). *Decolonizing Global Mental Health: The Psychiatrization of the Majority World*. New York and London: Routledge.

Mills, J. A. (2000). *Control: A History of Behavioral Psychology* (New edition). New York: NYU Press.

Milton, D. (2016). Tracing the influence of Fernand Deligny on autism studies. *Disability & Society, 31*(2), 285–289. doi:10.1080/09687599.2016.1161975.

Milton, D. E. M. (2014). So what exactly are autism interventions intervening with? *Good Autism Practice, 15*(2), 6–14.

Mirowski, P. (2015, March). What is science critique? Part 1: Lessig, Latour. Keynote address at the Workshop on the Changing Political Economy of Research and Innovation, UCSD, San Diego, CA. Retrieved from https://www.academia.edu/ 11571148/What_is_Science_Critique_Part_1_Lessig

Mittelstadt, B. D., Allo, P., Taddeo, M., Wachter, S., & Floridi, L. (2016). The ethics of algorithms: Mapping the debate. *Big Data & Society, 3*(2), 2053951716679679. doi:10.1177/2053951716679679.

Molko, R. (2018, July 20). *The Benefits of Neurodiversity in the Workplace.* ForbesBooks. Retrieved from https://forbesbooks.com/the-benefits-of-neurodiversity-in-the-workplace/.

Morton, T. (2017). *Humankind: Solidarity with Nonhuman People.* London and New York: Verso.

Moore, J. (2010). Behaviorism and the stages of scientific activity. *The Behavior Analyst, 33*(1), 47–63.

Nadesan, M. (2013). Autism: Profit, risk, and bare life. In J. Davidson & M. Orsini (eds.), *Worlds of Autism: Across the Spectrum of Neurological Difference.* Minneapolis: University of Minnesota Press.

National Institute of Mental Health. *NIMH Data Archive.* Retrieved January 14, 2020, from https://nda.nih.gov/about.html.

Neumeier, S. M., & Brown, L. X. Z. (2020). Torture in the name of treatment: The mission to stop the shocks in the age of deinstitutionalization. In S. K. Kapp (Ed.), *Autistic Community and the Neurodiversity Movement: Stories from the Frontline* (pp. 195–210). Singapore: Springer. doi:10.1007/978-981-13-8437-0_14.

Nevin, J. A. (1999). Analyzing Thorndike's law of effect: The question of stimulus—Response bonds. *Journal of the Experimental Analysis of Behavior, 72*(3), 447–450. doi:10.1901/jeab.1999.72-447.

Nik-Khah, E. (2017, October). *Neoliberalism, "Molecular Science," and the Future of Medicine.* Paper presented at the Taming the Pharmakon, Rome, Italy.

Novella, E. J. (2010). Mental health care and the politics of inclusion: A social systems account of psychiatric deinstitutionalization. *Theoretical Medicine and Bioethics, 31*(6), 411–427.

Ogilvie, B. (2013). Afterword. In S. Alvarez de Toledo (Ed.), *Cartes et lignes d'erre/ Maps and wander lines: Traces du réseau de Fernand Deligny.* Paris: L'Arachnéen.

Ortega, F. (2009). The cerebral subject and the challenge of neurodiversity. *BioSocieties, 4*(4), 425–445.

Osbeck, L. (2004). Asperger syndrome and capitalist social character. *Critical Psychology, 11,* 50–67.

Osbeck, L. (2018). *Values in Psychological Science: Re-imagining Epistemic Priorities at a New Frontier.* Cambridge, MA: Cambridge University Press.

Patil, T., & Giordano, J. (2010). On the ontological assumptions of the medical model of psychiatry: Philosophical considerations and pragmatic tasks. *Philosophy, Ethics, and Humanities in Medicine, 5*(1), 3. https://doi.org/10.1186/1747-5341-5-3.

References

Panksepp, J. (Ed.). (2004). *Textbook of Biological Psychiatry*. Hoboken, NJ: Wiley-Liss.

Parker, I. (2014). Madness and justice. *Journal of Theoretical and Philosophical Psychology, 34*(1), 28–40. doi:10.1037/a0032841.

Parsons, S., Yuill, N., Good, J., & Brosnan, M. (2019). 'Whose agenda? Who knows best? Whose voice?' Co-creating a technology research roadmap with autism stakeholders. *Disability & Society*, 1–34. doi:10.1080/09687599.2019.1624152.

Pew Research Center. (2015). "Child Poverty Rates, by Race and Ethnicity." Retrieved June 15, 2017, from www.pewresearch.org/fact-tank/2015/07/14/black-child-poverty-rate-holds-steady-even-as-other-groups-see-declines/ft_15-06-30_poverty_310px/.

Pias, C. (Ed.). (2016). *Cybernetics: The Macy Conferences 1946–1953. The Complete Transactions* (Revised edition). Zürich and Berlin: Diaphanes.

Pickering, A. (2016). *Ronald R. Kline: The Cybernetics Moment: Or Why We Call Our Age the Information Age*. Baltimore: Johns Hopkins University Press.

Pickersgill, M. D. (2013). Debating DSM-5: diagnosis and the sociology of critique. *Journal of Medical Ethics*. doi:10.1136/medethics-2013-101762.

Pilecki, B. C., Clegg, J. W., & McKay, D. (2011). The influence of corporate and political interests on models of illness in the evolution of the DSM. *European Psychiatry, 26*(3), 194–200.

Pinto, A. T. (2014). The pigeon in the machine: The concept of control in behaviourism and cybernetics. *Manifesta Journal, 18*, 65–73.

Pitts-Taylor, V. (2019). Neurobiologically poor? Brain phenotypes, inequality, and biosocial determinism. *Science, Technology, & Human Values*. doi:10.1177/0162243919841695.

Potenza, M. N. (2014). Non-substance addictive behaviors in the context of DSM-5. *Addictive Behaviors, 39*(1). doi:10.1016/j.addbeh.2013.09.004.

Remington, A. (2015, April 14). *Why employing autistic people makes good business sense*. The Conversation. Retrieved January 9, 2020, from http://theconversation.com/why-employing-autistic-people-makes-good-business-sense-39948.

Roberts, J. L. (2017). *Trauma and the Ontology of the Modern Subject* (1st edition). New York: Routledge.

Rollin, H. R. (1990). The dark before the dawn. *Journal of Psychopharmacology, 4*(3), 109–114.

Rollins, P. R., Campbell, M., Hoffman, R. T., & Self, K. (2015). A community-based early intervention program for toddlers with autism spectrum disorders. *Autism: The International Journal of Research and Practice*. doi:10.1177/1362361315577217.

Rose, N., & Abi-Rached, J. M. (2013). *Neuro: The New Brain Sciences and the Management of the Mind*. Princeton, NJ: Princeton University Press.

Rosenbaum, L. (2017). Swallowing a spy—The potential uses of digital adherence monitoring. *New England Journal of Medicine, 378* (2), 101–103.

Russell, G. (2020). Critiques of the neurodiversity movement. In S. K. Kapp (Ed.), *Autistic Community and the Neurodiversity Movement: Stories from the Frontline* (pp. 287–303). Singapore: Springer. doi:10.1007/978-981-13-8437-0_21.

References

Schmidt, R., Leventhal, D. K., Mallet, N., Chen, F., & Berke, J. D. (2013). Canceling actions involves a race between basal ganglia pathways. *Nature Neuroscience*, *16*(8), 1118–1124. doi:10.1038/nn.3456.

Schultz, D. P., & Schultz, S. E. (2015). *A History of Modern Psychology*. Boston, MA: Cengage Learning.

Scott B. (2016) Cybernetic foundations for psychology. *Constructivist Foundations*, *11*(3), 509–517. Retrieved from http://constructivist.info/11/3/509.

Seidel, K. (2020). Neurodiversity.Com: A decade of advocacy. In S. K. Kapp (Ed.), *Autistic Community and the Neurodiversity Movement: Stories from the Frontline* (pp. 89–107). Singapore: Springer. doi:10.1007/978-981-13-8437-0_7.

Shannon, C. E. (1971). *The Mathematical Theory of Communication* (W. Weaver, Ed.; 16th Printing edition). Urbana, IL: The University of Illinois Press.

Shorter, E. (1998). *A History of Psychiatry: From the Era of the Asylum to the Age of Prozac* (1st edition). New York: Wiley.

Shorter, E. (2015). The history of nosology and the rise of the diagnostic and statistical manual of mental disorders. *Dialogues in Clinical Neuroscience*, *17*(1), 59–67.

Simondon, G. (2007). *L'individuation psychique et collective*. Paris: Aubier.

Simondon, G. (2013). Technical mentality. In A. D. Boever (Trans.), *Gilbert Simondon: Being and Technology*. Edinburgh: Edinburgh University Press.

Simondon, G. (2017). *On the Mode of Existence of Technical Objects* (C. Malaspina & J. Rogove, Trans.; 1st edition). Minneapolis: University of Minnesota Press.

Skinner, B. F. (1953). *Science and Human Behavior*. New York: Macmillan.

Skinner, B. F. (1957). *Verbal Behavior*. New York: D. Appleton-Century.

Skinner, B. F. (1984). The shame of American education. *American Psychologist*, *39*(9), 947–954.

Skinner, B. F. (2005). *Walden Two* (Reprint edition). New York: Hackett Publishing Company, Inc.

Skott-Myhre, H. A. (2015). Marx, ideology and the unconscious. *Annual Review of Critical Psychology*, *12*, 59–64.

Skott-Myhre, H. A. and Taylor, C. (2011). Autism: Schizo of postmodern capital. *Deleuze Studies*, 35–48.

Smith, A. (1982). In A. Skinner (Ed.), *The Wealth of Nations: Books I-III* (new edition). London: Penguin Classics.

Smith, K. (2012). From dividual and individual selves to porous subjects. *The Australian Journal of Anthropology*, *23*(1), 50–64. https://doi.org/10.1111/j.1757-6547.2012.00167.x

Spring, B. (2007). Evidence-based practice in clinical psychology: What it is, why it matters; what you need to know. *Journal of Clinical Psychology*, *63*(7), 611–631. https://doi.org/10.1002/jclp.20373

Star, S. L., & Griesemer, J. R. (1989). Institutional ecology, 'Translations' and boundary objects: amateurs and professionals in Berkeley's Museum of Vertebrate Zoology, 1907–39. *Social Studies of Science*, *19*(3), 387–420. https://doi.org/10.1177/030631289019003001.

Stroul, B. A., Blau, G. M., & Sondheimer, D. L. (2008). Systems of care: A strategy to transform children's mental health care. In B. A. Stroul & G. M. Blau (Eds.),

The system of care handbook: Transforming mental health services for children, youth, and families (pp. 3–23). Paul H Brookes Publishing.

Sugarman, J. (2015). Neoliberalism and psychological ethics. *Journal of Theoretical and Philosophical Psychology, 35*(2), 103–116. https://doi.org/10.1037/a0038960

Szasz, T. S. (2010). *The Myth of Mental Illness: Foundations of a Theory of Personal Conduct* (50th Anniversary, Updated edition). New York: Harper Perennial.

Tabb, K. (2015). Psychiatric progress and the assumption of diagnostic discrimination. *Philosophy of Science, 82*(5), 1047–1058. doi:10.1086/683439.

Teo, T. (2018). Homo neoliberalus: From personality to forms of subjectivity. *Theory & Psychology, 28*(5), 581–599. doi:10.1177/0959354318794899.

Thelen, E. (1985). Expression as action: a motor perspective of the transition from spontaneous to instrumental behaviors. In G. Zivin (Ed.), *The Development of Expressive Behavior* (pp. 221–248). Orlando: Academic Press. https://doi.org/10.1016/B978-0-12-781780-4.50015-X

Thomas, F., Hansford, L., Ford, J., Hughes, S., Wyatt, K., McCabe, R., & Byng, R. (April, 2019). *Poverty, pathology and pills*. DeSTRESS PROJECT Final Report. Retrieved from http://DeSTRESSproject.org.uk/wp-content/uploads/2019/05/Final-report-8-May-2019-FT.pdf.

Thorndike, E. (1911). *Animal Intelligence*. Macmillan.

Tighe J. (1992). The legal art of psychiatric diagnosis: searching for reliability. In C. Rosenberg & J. Golden (Eds.), *Framing Disease* (pp. 206–226). New Brunswick, NJ: Rutgers University Press.

Tiqqun. (2010). *The Cybernetic Hypothesis*. Retrieved from https://theanarchistlibrary.org/library/tiqqun-the-cybernetic-hypothesis.

Tsou, J. Y. (2015). DSM-5 and psychiatry's second revolution: Descriptive vs. theoretical approaches to psychiatric classification. In S. Demazeux & P. Singy (Eds.), *The DSM-5 in Perspective: Philosophical Reflections on the Psychiatric Babel* (pp. 43–62). Netherlands: Springer. https://doi.org/10.1007/978-94-017-9765-8_3

U.S. Department of Health and Human Services. (2011). *Autism Research Database—Project Details | IACC*. Retrieved January 14, 2020, from https://iacc.hhs.gov/funding/data/project-details/?projectId=6129&fy=2011.

Umpleby, S. A. (2008). A short history of cybernetics in the United States. *Österreichische Zeitschrift für Geschichtswissenschaften, 19*, 28–40.

Unger, S. H. (1995). Hazards, critical races, and metastability. *IEEE Transactions on Computers, 44*(6), 754–768. doi:10.1109/12.391185.

van Bruggen, J. M., Kirschner, P. A., & Jochems, W. (2002). External representation of argumentation in CSCL and the management of cognitive load. *Learning and Instruction, 12*(1), 121–138. doi:10.1016/S0959-4752(01)00019-6.

Volkmar, F. R., & Reichow, B. (2013). Autism in DSM-5: Progress and challenges. *Molecular Autism, 4*, 13. https://doi.org/10.1186/2040-2392-4-13

von Foerster, H. (2007). *Understanding: Essays on Cybernetics and Cognition*. New York: Springer Science & Business Media.

von Neumann, J. (1948/1951). The general and logical theory of automata. *Cerebral Mechanisms in Behavior. The Hixon Symposium*. New York, NY: John Wiley & Sons, Inc.

Walker, N. (1956). Freud and homeostasis. *The British Journal for the Philosophy of Science, VII*(25), 61–72. doi:10.1093/bjps/VII.25.61.

Walker, N. (2014, September 27). Neurodiversity: Some basic terms & definitions. *NEUROCOSMOPOLITANISM*. Retrieved from https://neurocosmopolitanism.com/neurodiversity-some-basic-terms-definitions/.

Watson, J. B. (1913). Psychology as the behaviorist views it. *Psychological Review, 20*, 158–177.

Wazana, A., Bresnahan, M., & Kline, J. (2007). The autism epidemic: Fact or artifact? *Journal of the American Academy of Child & Adolescent Psychiatry, 46*(6), 721–730. doi:10.1097/chi.0b013e31804a7f3b.

Whitaker, R. (2019). *Mad in America: Bad Science, Bad Medicine, and the Enduring Mistreatment of the Mentally Ill* (Revised edition). New York: Basic Books.

Whitaker, R., & Cosgrove, L. (2015). *Psychiatry under the Influence*. New York: Palgrave. doi:10.1057/9781137516022_6.

Wiener, N. (1965). *Cybernetics: Or the Control and Communication in the Animal and the Machine* (2nd edition). Cambridge, MA: The MIT Press (Original work published 1948).

Wiener, N. (1989). *The Human Use of Human Beings: Cybernetics and Society* (New edition). New York: Free Association Books.

Willey, L. H. (1999). *Pretending to be Normal: Living with Asperger's Syndrome* (1st edition). London, Philadelphia: Jessica Kingsley Publishers.

Williams, R. W. (2005). Politics and self in the age of digital re(pro)ducibility. *Fast Capitalism, 1.1*. Retrieved from http://www.fastcapitalism.com

Winnicott, D. W. (1953). Transitional objects and transitional phenomena—A study of the first not-me possession. *International Journal of Psycho-Analysis, 34*, 89–97.

Woods, R. (2017). Pathological demand avoidance: My thoughts on looping effects and commodification of autism. *Disability & Society, 32*(5), 753–758. doi:10.1080/09687599.2017.1308705.

Zuboff, S. (2019). *The Age of Surveillance Capitalism: The Fight for a Human Future at the New Frontier of Power* (1st edition). New York: PublicAffairs.

Zucker, K. J. & Spitzer, R. L. (2005). Was the gender identity disorder of childhood diagnosis introduced into DSM-III as a backdoor maneuver to replace homosexuality? A historical note. *Journal of Sex and Marital Therapy, 31*, 31–42.

INDEX

Alcoholics Anonymous (AA) 32–34
Amazon 105–106
American Psychiatric Association (APA) 21, 82–83
Angell, James Rowland 46
Anti-Oedipus 146
anti-psychiatry 81, 140, 142
Aristotle 11
artificial intelligence (AI) 12, 22–23, 43, 61, 79, 103
attention economy 109
attention-deficit hyperactive disorder (ADHD) 94–96, 116
autism: the concept of 94–95, 121, 126, 134, 140–144; the diagnosis of (ASD) 94, 98, 121, 126, 134–135; as a social identity 121–122, 139

Barad, Karen 107
Bateson, Gregory 26, 32–35, 37, 39, 67, 73
behaviorism 3–4, 46, 48, 55–56, 63–66, 70–71, 112
Bernays, Edward 55
biomedical model 5–6, 21, 78–79, 82, 88, 99–100
boundary objects 19–20, 115
Bourdieu, Pierre 118
brainsets 69, 71–72

Breuer, Josef 46
British Psychological Society 21
Brown, Lydia X. Z. 137, 141–142
Bruner, Jerome 66

capitalism 9, 11, 34, 106, 120, 132, 142
Carter, Jimmy 83
Central Intelligence Agency (CIA) 25, 35–36
Charcot, Jean-Martin 46
Châtelet, Gilles 110
China's social credit system 104–105, 111
Chomsky, Noam 64–65
cognitive neuroscience 3–4, 48, 56, 65–66, 72–74, 86, 109, 112, 128
cognitive-behavioral therapy (CBT) 49, 54
Coleman, Gabriella 130–132
collective assemblages of enunciation 6, 144
computational models of the mind *see* information processing model
computerize axial tomography (CAT) 68
Cybernetics: Communication and control in the animal and the machine (Wiener) 25
cybernetics: and the CIA 35–36; concept of information 16, 78–79;

critiques of 36, 39, 105–106, 125, 144; and control 2, 20, 30, 32, 35, 38–39, 133; epistemology of 5–6, 15, 21, 26, 28, 30, 38–39, 50–51, 56, 125; first-order 26, 31–33; history of 2–3, 7, 15, 18, 23, 25–26, 31, 36, 47, 61, 66–67, 73, 85, 107, 109, 124, 133; metaphors vii, 17–18, 20, 26, 107–108; second-order 32–35, 107; technologies 15, 18, 39
cyborg 15–16, 112, 143–144

Darwin, Charles 34, 101
data-capitalism 109
Davar, Bhargavi 120
deinstitutionalization 5, 19, 77–78, 80–82, 85, 128, 133, 139
Deleuze, Gilles vii, 2–3, 7, 16, 109–110, 117–118
Deligny, Fernand 125–127, 129, 142
Descartes, Rene 11–12, 14–16, 38, 50, 57, 62
desiring-machines 146
deterritorialization 35, 117
Dewey, John 46
Diagnostic and Statistical Manual for Mental Disorders (DSM): alternatives to 14, 21, 99, 127; and biological mechanisms 78, 83, 86–87; changes across editions of 5, 82–83; clinical value of 4, 116; diagnoses within 19, 21, 137, 142; first two editions 81, 84; fourth edition 83, 91; fifth edition 19, and insurance reimbursement 90; and operationalization 84, 88, 91, 108, 116; and the pharmaceutical industry 91; and social work 90; third edition 82
dialectical-behavioral therapy (DBT) 50
digital computers 13, 30, 66–67, 73, 79
Donders, Frans 70–71
driveconcept 48, 53, 59–60

electroencephalography (EEG) 68
entropy 28–30
Erickson, Milton 67
Evans, Meg 95, 141
evidence-based practice 22–23, 79, 116

Facebook 105–106
Fechner, Gustav 46

Food and Drug Administration (FDA) 80, 137
Foerster, Hans von 26, 31–32, 75
Foucault, Michel 109
Frank, Lawrence 35, 67
Fremont-Smith, Frank 25, 44, 67
functional magnetic resonance imaging (fMRI) 68, 70

Giddens, Anthony 92
global mental health movements viii, 36, 92, 117, 120
Google 105–106
Group Psychology and the Analysis of the Ego (Freud) 54
Guattari, Felix viii, 7, 115, 117

hacking 6, 129–132, 139, 144
Hayles, Katherine N. 107
Haraway, Donna 13, 16, 107
hearing voices network vii, 6, 144, 146
Hebb, Donald 106
Helmholtz, Hermann von 46
Hull, Clarke 56, 59–61, 65
The Human Use of Human Beings: Cybernetics and Society (Wiener) 28

individuation vii, 3, 7, 41, 43, 52, 55, 112–113, 115, 124, 128, 131
information economy 109
information processing model 17, 30–31, 107, 119
Insel, Thomas 84–86, 96
institutionalized psychiatry 19, 80–81, 126
International Classification for Diseases (ICD) 21, 78, 108
internet 23, 49, 106, 129, 131, 140

Josiah Macy Foundation 25, 31
Judge Rotenberg Center 137

Kennedy, J. F. 81, 83
Kubie, Lawrence 67

late-capitalism 109
Liddell, Howard 67

McCulloch, Warren 67, 79, 82, 107
Macy conferences 25–26, 30–31, 34–36, 67

mad pride 139, 146
magnetic resonance imaging (MRI) 69–70
Malabou, Catherine 74–75, 135
Mead, Margaret 26, 32, 35, 67
Microsoft 105–106, 122
Miller, George A. 66
Mills, John 55
Milton, Damian 94, 126
myths of auto-individuation vii, 4–6, 26, 45, 55, 78–79, 95, 111–112, 117–118, 124, 133

National Institute of Mental Health (NIMH) 84, 97
neo-Kraepelinian models 82, 101
neoliberalism 89, 96–97, 103, 105–106, 109, 121, 132
network as a mode of being 6, 124–125
network models of psychopathology 99, 101, 103, 110, 118
Neumann, John von 107
Neumeier, Shain 137, 141–142
neurodiversity viii, 6, 121–122, 126, 135, 139–145

Oedipal complex 41–42
operant conditioning 49, 62–66

Pavlov, Ivan 56–58, 75
positron-emission tomography (PET) 68–74, 87
Power Threat Meaning Framework 21
psychoanalysis 35, 43, 48–57, 73
psychopharmaceuticals 81–83, 87–88

Reagan, Ronald 83
Research Domain Criteria (RDoC) 84–86, 101

Rhett's syndrome 83
Rosenblueth, Arturo 67

Schelling, Freidrich 50
Seidel, Kathleen 140
Seven Psychologies (Heidbredder) 45
Shannon, Claude 66–67, 73, 134
The Shock Doctrine (Klein) 106
Sigmund, Freud 11–13, 40–41, 43, 45, 48–56, 65, 81, 115, 132
Simondon, Gilbert 3, 6–7, 15, 26–27, 36–42, 61–62, 128, 144
Skinner, B. F. 13, 29, 55–56, 62–66, 105, 137
social capital 118–120
social media 6, 8, 13, 113
societies of control vii, 2, 43, 109–113, 118, 125, 133
Spinoza, Baruch 129, 145
SSRIs 88
surveillance capitalism 109

Thorndike, John 56, 58–60
transindividuation 6, 36, 41–42, 47, 112, 144, 146

the unconscious 4, 13, 48–53, 54–56, 65

Watson, John 46, 55–56
Wiener, Norbert 25–26, 28–33, 37, 39, 67, 71, 133
World Federation of Mental Health 35–36
World Health Organization 21, 36
Wundt, Wilhelm 46

x-ray 68

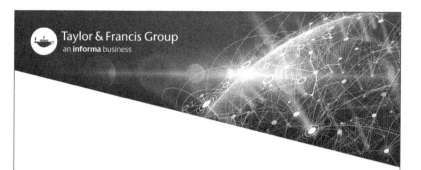